GUIDE FOR
BLESSINGS

PREPARING PARISH WORSHIP™

MICHAEL KWATERA, OSB
DOLORES MARTINEZ
D. TODD WILLIAMSON

LITURGY
TRAINING
PUBLICATIONS

Nihil Obstat	*Imprimatur*
Deacon Daniel G. Welter, JD	Most Rev. Robert G. Casey
Chancellor	Vicar General
Archdiocese of Chicago	Archdiocese of Chicago
March 10, 2022	March 10, 2022

GUIDE FOR CELEBRATING BLESSINGS © 2022 Archdiocese of Chicago: Liturgy Training Publications, 3949 South Racine Avenue, Chicago, IL 60609; 800-933-1800; fax: 800-933-7094; email: orders@ltp.org; website: www.LTP.org. All rights reserved.

This book is part of the *Preparing Parish Worship*™ series.

This book was edited by Danielle A. Noe. Michael A. Dodd was the production editor, Anna Manhart was the series designer, and Matthew B. Clark was the production artist and cover designer.

The image on page 3 is by Le Second Empire à Orsay; courtesy Wikimedia Commons. Art on page vi © Martin Erspamer, OSB. Photos on pages 6 and 19 courtesy of St. Mary's Basilica, St. Paul, MN; pages 10, 53, and 51 by Karen Callaway, © *Catholic Chicago/Catolico*; pages 15, 22, and 56 © Liturgy Training Publications; pages 21, 25, 29, 31, 24, 26, 61, and 64 © John Zich; page 46 courtesy St. Raphael Catholic Church, Naperville, IL; page 47 by Lori Reynolds, courtesy Sonoita Vineyards, Elgin, AZ; page 66 © Cranes Photography; page 70 © Juan Alberto Castillo; and page 73 © Rush Photo and Video.

26 25 24 23 22   1 2 3 4 5

Printed in the United States of America

Library of Congress Control Number: 2022933915

ISBN: 978-1-61671-421-5

EGCB

CONTENTS

PREFACE

L et go of me," Peter begged, his sun-beaten face fixed with an inappropriate scowl. Then, "Please," he added meekly, suddenly remembering that if he wanted to talk about Jesus, he'd better act like Jesus.

Tertius, however, was not letting go. "Thank you, thank you, thank you!" he exclaimed. "You healed me! I can stand! I can walk! I can jump!"—all of which he demonstrated while clinging not only to Peter but to John as well.[1] John laughed out loud at Peter's predicament. Meanwhile, a crowd was growing.

"Look," Peter reasoned with the man, "I'm excited too. I'm happy you can use your legs, but I'd like to use my arms."

"This is the first time," Tertius crowed, "the first time in my entire life that I can walk!"

Lois and Alexandra, approaching Solomon's Portico in the Temple area at the three o'clock hour of prayer,[2] noticed the commotion. How could they not? Three adult men, one embracing the other two with superhuman strength, one struggling to push away, and the third laughing uncontrollably.

"Wait a minute," Lois said to Alexandra, her eyes growing wider. "Isn't that . . . ? No. No, it can't be."

"What?" asked Alexandra. "Who?"

"That man in the middle!" Lois nearly shouted. "It's Tertius!"

Alexandra looked at Lois as if she were out of her mind. "Tertius!" she exclaimed. Then Alexandra started laughing. "Oh, come on, Lois. That's ridiculous. Tertius has been crippled from birth. His aging parents still carry him down to the Beautiful Gate every day to beg for alms.[3] They're clever. They know we come to this holy ground because we want God to be pleased with our actions. They put a crippled man right in our path so that we have to choose between being kind to him—in hopes of pleasing God—and

---

1. See Acts of the Apostles 3:8.
2. See Acts 3:1.
3. See Acts 3:2.

ignoring him at our own peril. Tertius is annoying. He is clever. But his infirmity is real. He cannot walk."

"It's him," Lois declared, as the three men disappeared into the Temple.[4]

Phaedra walked up to them. "I saw it all. Tertius did what he always does with everyone who passes by, whether he knows them or not. These men are strangers to us, but they seem to be close friends with each other. One is called Peter. The other is named John. Tertius is not shy with anyone. As soon as they arrived, he asked both of them for alms. Peter looked at him fiercely. I thought he was going to scold him. But then Peter said, 'Look at us.[5] I have neither silver nor gold, but what I do have I give you: in the name of Jesus Christ the Nazorean, rise and walk.'[6] Then with his right hand he grabbed Tertius by the arm and pulled him up on his feet.[7] Tertius stood on his own—on his own two feet! I could hardly believe my eyes. Then he did not wait to test his strength. He walked, leaped up, and jumped around as happy and playful as a six-year old child. He praised God just like the others who come regularly to the Temple at this hour. Then Tertius came back to Peter and John and threw his arms around them. He still hasn't let go."[8]

Alexandra asked, "Wait a minute. Who is this 'Jesus Christ the Nazorean'?"

As if on cue, Peter, still in the grip of Tertius, who was still hauling John around as well, appeared at Solomon's Portico. Many people were now rushing there to see the miraculous healing with their own eyes.[9] In spite of Tertius, an awkward appendage on his arm, Peter resigned himself to begin the speech he had been longing to give the crowd mustering around him.

"Why are you amazed at this?[10] The God of our ancestors has glorified his servant Jesus whom you handed over and denied in Pilate's presence.[11] And by faith in his name, this man, whom you see and know, his name has made strong.[12] You are the children of the prophets and of the covenant that God made with your ancestors when he said to Abraham, 'in your offspring all the families of the earth shall be blessed.'"[13]

---

4. See Acts 3:8.
5. See Acts 3:4.
6. See Acts 3:6.
7. See Acts 3:7.
8. See Acts 3:11.
9. See Acts 3:11.
10. Acts 3:12.
11. See Acts 3:13.
12. See Acts 3:16.
13. Acts 3:25.

"Blessed," said Alexandra to Lois. "Well, yes, I have always felt blessed in my life. I feel blessed for my good health, that my parents helped me, and that my children never had to suffer as Tertius did. The gift of faith has also made me feel blessed."

Peter said, "For you first, God raised up his servant."[14] Lois remarked, "He must be referring to this Jesus."

Peter continued, "and sent him to bless you by turning each of you from your evil ways."[15]

Jesus came to bless.

"Yes," said Phaedra. "That is how I feel. I feel that God has been continually at my side, turning me from choosing what is evil and toward God's will."

Lois said, "God sent prophets into the world to announce God's purpose and to turn us from sin. But this Jesus sounds different."

"Yes," said Alexandra. "He came to bless."

The followers of Jesus continue to seek and give blessings in his name. Whenever they do, they continue the purpose of his life: God sent Jesus to bless.

—Paul Turner

PAUL TURNER is pastor of the Cathedral of the Immaculate Conception in Kansas City, Missouri. and the director of the Office of Divine Worship for the Diocese of Kansas City–St. Joseph. He holds a doctorate in sacred theology from Sant'Anselmo in Rome and has published many pastoral and liturgical resources.

14. Acts 3:26.
15. Acts 3:26.

WELCOME

Welcome to *Guide for Celebrating Blessings*. This resource will be of help to almost any parish minister for understanding and implementing the many orders of blessing found in the *Book of Blessings* approved for use in the dioceses of the United States. Intended to make orders of blessing accessible, this book gives guidance and direction for the preparation and celebration of these important rituals.

The *Book of Blessings* is, perhaps, one of the best-kept secrets in the collection of rites and rituals of the Catholic Church. It would be difficult to find a richer or more inspirational pastoral resource, as it offers numerous ritual opportunities that may be adapted to specific circumstances. Useable in almost any setting (school, religious education classes, parish meetings, initiation gatherings, adult faith formation, and during Mass), this ritual book provides an order of blessing complete with prayers, readings, intercessions, and directions for how the celebrations should take place. As a source of ritual prayer, it includes blessings for almost any situation: children, students and teachers, a new library, boats and fishing gear, animals . . . you get the idea!

About This Book

Beginning with a historical overview of the role of blessings within the life of the Church, this resource reflects upon the spirituality and theology expressed by the liturgical action of blessing. The theological and historical overview will help situate the celebrations of blessings within the overall liturgical life of the parish and parish school.

Following the theological and historical overview is a pastoral guide to the *Book of Blessings* itself. This section outlines the various sections, chapters, and appendixes of the ritual book and provides an overview of the basic structure of an order of blessing, identifying its parts and various liturgical elements. This section concludes with an exploration of the roles and ministries that are exercised in the celebration of a blessing. Each of the orders found in the *Book of Blessings* has a number of options that can be used depending on the circumstances, the place where the blessing is being celebrated, and who is presiding at or leading the blessing. This section offers direction and suggestions when addressing these options. This material provides a solid example for the preparation and celebration of any of the orders of blessings and makes recommendations for particular adaptation. For the purposes of this resource, pastoral commentary cannot be provided for every blessing found in the *Book of Blessings*. The authors have chosen to review those blessings that are most often celebrated in the parish. The pastoral guidance can be easily applied to other blessings.

As with other books in the *Preparing Parish Worship*™ series, *Guide for Celebrating Blessings* identifies frequently asked questions that may surface in the preparation or celebration of an order of blessing. The answers respect the rubrics and liturgical norms of blessings and take into account the pastoral realities in which any blessing may be celebrated.

Finally, the resources section and the glossary offer further direction and guidance for pastoral ministers responsible for the preparation of an order of blessing. The resources chapter provides an annotated bibliography for those who would like to do further reading on the topic of blessings, and the glossary identifies various terms and phrases encountered in blessings and other liturgies and rituals.

About the Authors

REV. MICHAEL KWATERA, OSB, is a monk of St. John's Abbey in Collegeville, Minnesota, and serves as its director of liturgy. He holds a PHD in theology from the University of Notre Dame. He has served as pastor of several rural parishes and as a teacher of Christian worship at St. John's University in Collegeville, Minnesota, and also as a faculty resident in an undergraduate residence there. He has regularly celebrated the Eucharist with the Franciscan Sisters of Little Falls, Minnesota. Among his publications are several books for liturgical ministers, prayer books, and articles in liturgical journals. From 2009 to 2019 his monthly question-and-answer column on liturgical topics appeared in *The Visitor*, the St. Cloud diocesan newspaper.

DOLORES MARTINEZ serves as director for worship in the Archdiocese of San Antonio. She has also served as an independent liturgical consultant and formator in liturgy and music, and as a parish music minister. Dolores has music published by Oregon Catholic Press in the *Flor y Canto* hymnal and other collections, and articles published in *GIA Quarterly* (GIA). Dolores received her PHD in fine arts from Texas Tech University in Lubbock, Texas.

D. TODD WILLIAMSON is the director of the Office for Divine Worship of the Archdiocese of Chicago, a position he's held for twenty years. He is a speaker, author, and liturgist whose ministerial experience includes teaching and parish pastoral ministry. He is an adjunct faculty member of St. Mary of the Lake University in Mundelein, Illinois, and the Institute of Pastoral Studies of Loyola University, Chicago. He is the author of the 2007 and 2008 editions of *Sourcebook for Sundays, Seasons, and Weekdays: An Almanac of Parish Liturgy* (Liturgy Training Publications), and a contributor to subsequent editions. He is coauthor of *Great Is the Mystery: The Formational Power of Liturgy* (Liturgy Training Publications) and most recently he coauthored *Guide for Celebrating Christian Initiation with Adults* (Liturgy Training Publications).

The Theological and Historical Development of Blessings

"Blessed are you, Lord God of all creation . . ."

— The Liturgy of the Eucharist

reation: God's and ours. Today there is renewed emphasis on creation as the cooperative action between God and humanity,[1] but earlier ages glimpsed this truth more clearly. In the windows, friezes, and mural decorations of medieval cathedrals we often find the figures of men or women engaged in some rather ordinary tasks: plowing, receiving grain at the mill, bleaching a length of cloth, spinning, binding up sheaves of wheat. The artist was emphasizing a fundamental truth: by faithfully fulfilling one's daily work, one cooperates with God's plan for creation.

Such artistic representations only image the real synthesis between religion and life effected in the Church's blessings for the many circumstances and activities of human life. The Church blessed homes, stables and barns, fields and vineyards, pastures and animals.

> The source from whom every good gift comes is God, who is above all, blessed for ever.
>
> — Book of Blessings, 1

The Church blessed agricultural produce: eggs and honey, butter and cheese, wine and beer. Such prayers reflected a sacramental approach to the activities that produced these material things by pointing to the greater reality of God's work in which they shared.

No one had a better awareness of this than Celtic Christians, the peoples of Wales, Scotland, and Ireland, whose Gaelic prayers and blessings were gathered and edited in various collections at the turn of the nineteenth century. Among the Celts, God's presence was keenly felt in creation, and even more in the daily round of domestic tasks and at the most important moments of

---

1. See Catherine Vincie, *Worship and the New Cosmology* (Collegeville, MN: Liturgical Press, 2014).

human life. Prayers of blessing marked all of these household settings and activities. For example:

> Bless, O God, the fire,
>   As Thou didst bless the Virgin;
> Bless, O God, the hearth,
>   As Thou didst bless the Sabbath.
> Bless, O God, the household,
>   According as Jesus said;
> Bless, O God, the family,
>   As becomes us to offer it.
> Bless, O God, the house,
>   Bless, O God, the fire,
> Bless, O God, the hearth;
>   Be Thyself our stay.
>   May the Being of Life bless,
>   May the Christ of love bless,
>   May the Spirit Holy bless
>   Each one and all,
>   Every one and all.[2]

The Church's blessings, some celebrated within the liturgy and some at other times, proliferated in the early Middle Ages as the Northern European peoples were converted to Christianity and came to believe in the surpassing power of the one true God. The almighty Lord of heaven and earth was called upon to render help and protection just as their previous gods had been. Over time, abuse and superstition crept in, especially in the later Middle Ages. For example, holy water and relics were used to treat illness in livestock and people, and church bells were rung to dispel storms. Slim, red candles were used during childbirth to protect against demons and other evil spirits.

When diocesan synods failed to stem such misuse of sacred things, Pope Paul V published an official *Rituale Romanum* for the universal Church (June 16, 1614), to which all diocesan rituals were to conform while still allowing for local adaptation in different parts of the world. This volume, with two expansions or revisions (1752, 1925), was retained until the Second Vatican Council.

The *Rituale Romanum* included the rites for all the sacraments and sacramentals that were not included in the missal or the breviary, and this

---

2. *The Celtic Vision: Prayers and Blessings from the Outer Hebrides*, ed. Esther de Waal (Liguori, MO: Liguori/Triumph, 2001; p. 75). Used with permission of Liguori Publications.

"The Blessing of the Wheat in Artois," painted by Jules Breton (1857), beautifully depicts a Eucharistic procession in a hayfield. Historically, the exposed sacrament would have been used in the act of blessing, and the community eagerly took part.

volume served as a useful companion for the parish priest. There were blessings for people, objects, and occasions: for agricultural products and the work of human hands, as well as prayers for favorable weather and for rain, for good crops and a bountiful harvest. There were special blessings, litanies, and processions against drought, flood, plague, and pestilence.

Canon Law identified two types of liturgical blessings: *constitutive*, which permanently dedicated a person or an object in service of the Church—for example, the consecration of a bishop or of an altar; and *invocative*, which asked God to assist those in need or who use blessed objects—for example, the blessing for sick persons or the blessing of an automobile. Some of these blessings in the *Rituale Romanum* reflected the industrial age, for example the Blessing of an Electric Dynamo in an electric power plant. These blessings were seen as a means to obtain temporal or spiritual help by sanctifying or consecrating a person, thing, or activity.

The *Rituale Romanum* reserved some blessings—for example, of farm machinery—to the clergy, but it extended unreserved blessings—for example, of farm animals—to lay persons. Many lay persons then, and perhaps even now, believed the priest's blessing to be more powerful and therefore preferable.

Perhaps adequate instruction of the faithful was lacking, and superstition revived in the seventeenth and eighteenth centuries. By the twentieth century, these prayers and blessings had become infrequent or nonexistent in many places. Their decline was already evident in the 1940s when authors such as Thomas Allen regretted the fact that "so many good Catholics living in rural communities do not make use of these blessings which refer to the land and the products of the soil."[3] Perhaps some feared that people were treating the Church's sacramentals as magic wands; perhaps some considered them to be unnecessary in the modern age.

The Second Vatican Council undertook to reevaluate and restore blessings, not in order to promote antiquarianism or nostalgia, but to recover spiritual riches so necessary for life today:

> The sacramentals [including blessings] are to be reviewed in the light of the primary criterion that the faithful must participate intelligently, actively and easily; the conditions of our own days must also be considered. When rituals are revised, in accord with art. 63, new sacramentals may also be added as the need for them becomes apparent.[4]

Among the study groups created by the Consilium[5] for the implementation of *Sacrosanctum concilium*, group number 23, entitled *De Rituale II*, had as its focus the revision of the sacramentals, and especially title IX of the *Rituale Romanum*, "On Blessings." Work began in 1970, but practically stopped in 1972. The efforts of two subsequent study groups resulted in the *Rituale Romanum: De Benedictionibus* that was promulgated by the Congregation for Divine Worship on May 31, 1984.

Two years earlier, the United States Bishops' Committee on the Liturgy had established a subcommittee on blessings to review an earlier draft of the Latin text and the English draft translation prepared by the International Committee on English in the Liturgy (ICEL). Their task was to formulate the various rites and blessings to be added to the English edition of the *Book of Blessings*. These were to be included as a result of the consultation of diocesan liturgical commissions conducted by the Committee on the Liturgy in 1984. On March 22, 1988, the National Conference of Catholic Bishops approved the English edition of the *Book of Blessings* for use in the dioceses of the United States. This edition, confirmed by the Apostolic See on January 27, 1989, includes forty-two new blessings proper to the United States. This English edition is the one required for use since December 4, 1989.

The content and arrangement of the *Book of Blessings* for the United States is found on the chart on page 5.

---

3. Thomas Allen, ᴏꜱʙ, "The Land and Sacramentals," *Land and Home* (September 1942): 2.

4. *Sacrosanctum concilium* (SC), 79.

5. Those charged with the task of implementing the liturgical reform called for by the Second Vatican Council.

Part I	Blessings Directly Pertaining to Persons
Part II	Blessings Related to Buildings and to Various Forms of Human Activity
Part III	Blessings of Objects That Are Designed or Erected for Use in Churches, Either in the Liturgy or in Popular Devotions
Part IV	Blessings of Articles Meant to Foster the Devotion of the Christian People
Part V	Blessings Related to Feasts and Seasons
Part VI	Blessings for Various Needs and Occasions
Appendix I	Order for the Installation of a Pastor
Appendix II	Solemn Blessings and Prayers over the People

The blessings included in the *Book of Blessings* rest on centuries of Christian practice, which itself is rooted in the Jewish euchological (prayer) tradition. For the ancient Israelites, praise and thanksgiving were two closely related aspects of divine worship, but they were not identical. To "bless" God was to "praise" God: "I will bless the LORD at all times, / his praise shall always be in my mouth."[6] To praise God was to participate in a sacred action whereby God's blessing, God's favor, came upon those in need. To receive God's blessing meant being saved from some crisis, danger, or need. And past deliverance became the basis for the Jewish people's hope and confidence that God would grant their present requests as well.

Thus, in the Jewish tradition of prayer, it is unthinkable to ask anything of God without first offering praise and thanksgiving for what God has already given. Such thinking is reflected in the traditional Jewish *berakah* ("blessing") form of prayer, which begins with an expression of praise ("Blessed are you, Lord our God"), followed by remembrance of God's saving deeds, request for present help, and a final expression of praise which is sealed by the "Amen." In answer, God would pour forth the sustaining power of life itself as growth, increase, success, fertility, and prosperity. God's blessing imparts all good gifts for body, soul, and spirit. Thus, in the Jewish tradition, blessings recognize and proclaim the goodness of creation and the providence of the Creator.

---

6. Psalm 34:2.

Blessings praise God for the gift of creation. Shown here is the blessing of animals at St. Mary's Basilica in Minneapolis, MN.

Human beings, made in the image of God, recognize and proclaim that all created things come from God, as they bless and thank God the giver.

The *Book of Blessings* explains:

> Whether God blessed the people himself or through the ministry of those who acted in his name, his blessing was always a promise of divine help, a proclamation of his favor, a reassurance of his faithfulness to the covenant he had made with his people. When in turn, others uttered blessings, they were offering praise to the one whose goodness and mercy they were proclaiming.[7]

Thus, blessings first and foremost are directed to praising God's majesty and goodness, but they are also directed to benefitting the people upon whom God wishes to bestow grace and favor.

This two-directional aspect of blessings is seen in Psalm 134, a "Song of Ascents" or pilgrimage song. In what is really a brief liturgy, pilgrims gather at the temple in Jerusalem at night, and exhort the priests and Levites about to begin their night watch to praise the Lord:

> O come, bless the LORD,
> all you servants of the LORD,
> You who stand in the house of the LORD
> throughout the nights.
> Lift up your hands toward the sanctuary,
> and bless the LORD[8].

---

7. *Book of Blessings* (BB), 6.
8. Psalm 134:1b–2.

GUIDE FOR CELEBRATING® BLESSINGS

God's ministers bless him by praising and thanking him and by offering him their reverent worship and service. We lack the actual words and songs of praise that they offer, but we have the blessing that they invoke upon the pilgrims in God's name and from his dwelling place, a blessing for safety on their way:

> May the LORD bless you from Zion,
> the Maker of heaven and earth.[9]

God is ever-blessing, ever-blest. In blessing God with our praise, we are blessed in our praising by receiving his gifts. God is ever-blessing—always bestowing divine grace and favor; and God is ever-blest—always and everywhere being praised by those who are graced and favored by God. "The Law, the Prophets, and the Psalms, interwoven in the liturgy of the Chosen People, recall these divine blessings and at the same time respond to them with blessings of praise and thanksgiving."[10] This is clearly seen in Psalm 72, which is filled with hope for the king-Messiah as Israel would desire him to be:

> May his name be forever;
> as long as the sun, may his name endure.
> May the tribes of the earth give blessings with his name;
> may all the nations regard him as favored.[11]

Christian faith sees every earthly and heavenly blessing most fully given in and through Jesus Christ, for all of creation has been transformed in him:

> Scripture attests that all the beings God has created and keeps in existence by his gracious goodness declare themselves to be blessings from him and should move us to bless him in return. This is above all true after the Word made flesh came to make all things holy by the mystery of his incarnation.[12]

In his introduction to the blessings in his 1964 translation of the 1952 edition of the *Roman Ritual*, Rev. Philip Weller wrote:

> In the Epistle to the Romans St. Paul records that the complete emancipation of creation will not be effected until the end of time. But ever since Our Lord transfigured lower creatures by employing them in sacramental ways— consider His use of bread, wine, water, oil, sacred signs—material things have been participating with Him and with man in divine worship. And

---

9. Psalm 134:3.
10. *Catechism of the Catholic Church* (CCC), 1081.
11. Psalm 72:17.
12. BB, 7.

where Christ left off, the Church continues. The consecration and transfiguration of the creatures is done through sacraments and sacramentals.[13]

The New Testament affirms that God's blessings in Jesus Christ are tasted in the present through material things but they are also to be fully and eternally enjoyed in the future.

The *Apostolic Tradition,* formerly attributed to Hippolytus (ca. AD 215), is witness to blessings of things during the celebration of the Eucharist: oil for the use of the sick and milk, honey, and water to be consumed by the newly baptized at Communion. The bishop is to pray this over cheese and olives:

> Sanctify this curdled milk
> by uniting us to your love.
> Grant too that this fruit of the olive tree
> may never lose its sweetness.
> It is a symbol of the abundance
> that you make flow from the tree (of the cross)
> to give life to those who hope in you.[14]

Bishop Serapion of Thmuis in the Nile Delta (d. ca. 362) included a blessing for the harvest in his *Euchology.*

Perhaps the Roman liturgy included the blessing of the fruits of the earth before the doxology at the conclusion of the Eucharistic Prayer so as to highlight the relationship of such blessings to the greatest of God's blessings: Christ himself, and his saving work, re-presented through sacramental signs in the Eucharist. These are the objects referred to in the closing words of Eucharistic Prayer I (the Roman Canon): "Through whom / [Christ] you continue to make all these good things, O Lord; / you sanctify them, fill them with life, / bless them, and bestow them upon us."

People in the New Testament era and Patristic age had a lively sense that evil spirits might be lurking in material things, and so blessings from that time have a pronounced exorcistic tone. But the Church's contemporary purpose and theology of blessing as reflected in the *Book of Blessings* is broader and more positive, for in these prayers we celebrate the goodness of God's creation and our God-given role in protecting and advancing it as the Creator intends. This is the spiritual universe of the *Book of Blessings,* for:

---

13. Philip T. Weller, *The Roman Ritual: Complete Edition* (Milwaukee, WI: Bruce, 1964), 386.

14. Luicen Deiss, cssp, *Springtime of the Liturgy,* trans. Matthew J. O'Connell (Collegeville, MN: Liturgical Press, 1979), 133.

The Church has a profound concern that the celebration of blessings should truly contribute to God's praise and glory and should serve to better God's people. In order that this intent of the Church might stand out more clearly, blessing formularies have, from age-old tradition, centered above all on glorifying God for his gifts, on imploring favors from him, and on restraining the power of evil in this world.[15]

At a time when many people feel powerless in facing difficult situations, blessings can open them to God's power to protect and save when human resources are lacking or inadequate. "By means of blessing we are called to share this divine power so that we may proclaim to the whole world the unfathomable marvels of God."[16] This is why the corporate strength that comes from celebrating blessings is more clearly seen within the liturgical assembly and why priority should be given to communal celebration of these blessings with the active participation of the assembly: "Communal celebration is in some cases obligatory, but in all cases more in accord with the character of liturgical prayer."[17] This is very different from thinking that persons, objects, or places are blessed if a priest simply makes the Sign of the Cross over them in the sacristy or rectory and sprinkles them with holy water. Indeed, the *Book of Blessings* declares that "to ensure active participation in the celebration and to guard against any danger of superstition, it is ordinarily not permissible to impart the blessing of any article or place merely through a sign of blessing and without either the word of God or any sort of prayer being spoken."[18]

Through its many forms of blessing, the Church "calls us to praise God, encourages us to implore his protection, exhorts us to seek his mercy by our holiness of life, and provides us with ways of praying that God will grant us the favors we ask."[19]

In our age that dallies with self-destruction, the Church's blessings summon us to celebrate creation as a divine gift and a human responsibility. In 1949, Mary Charity, OP, explained that "the Church through her blessings . . . tries to stir us to an acknowledgement of the right order between creature and Creator, co-worker and Master, . . . but by and large this

---

15. BB, 11.

16. Antonio Donghi, *Actions and Words: Symbolic Language of the Liturgy*, trans. William McDonough and Dominic Serra, ed. Mark Twomey and Elizabeth L. Montgomery (Collegeville, MN: Liturgical Press, 1997), 69.

17. BB, 16.

18. BB, 27.

19. BB, 9.

Blessings acknowledge God's sovereignty over creation and our dependence upon him.

integrated outlook has been replaced by man's possessiveness and claim to absolute dominion."[20] As we ask God's blessings on people and things in the prayers found in the *Book of Blessings*, we acknowledge God's sovereignty over creation and our human dependence on him.

To speak a blessing does not free something from the control of evil spirits or change it from something 'profane' into something 'sacred,' as though the objects themselves thereby could become bearers of some kind of extrinsic supernatural power."[21] Rather, it frees us from the demons of greed and materialism and helps conform our selfish attitudes to the divine will of the Creator. A horse really does not need a prayer of blessing and sprinkling with holy water; as a work of nature, it is fine just as it is. But we need to set it apart for our use by sacred words and gestures; we need to render to God our praise for the beauty and benefits it provides. We may even find ourselves more careful and reverent in its use, because we pledge ourselves to use God's creatures in a spirit of gratitude, love, and praise, according to God's plan for the universe. In celebrating blessings, the Church "praises the Lord and implores divine grace at important moments in the life of its members. At times, the Church also invokes blessings on objects and places connected with human occupations or activities and those related to the liturgy or to piety and popular devotions. But such blessings are invoked always

---

20. Mary Charity, OP, "Thanking for Harvests," *Orate Fratres* 23, no. 12 (November 6, 1949): 540.

21. Wagner, S. Mary Anthony, OSB, *The Sacred World of the Christian: Sensed in Faith* (Collegeville, MN: Liturgical Press, 1993), 110.

with a view to the people who use the objects to be blessed and frequent the places to be blessed."[22] And the blessings we celebrate and that spring from our celebration are to inspire and empower our action for the good of others. When we speak a "grace before meals," "we thank God for his loving care, and are ready to imitate him by our sincere concern for others: the blessing of food needs to be followed by the sharing of food with others who need it."[23] This is the truth expressed in the song of the Benedictine monk of Weston Priory, Gregory Norbet: "Simple is the truth that our love cannot be real unless we choose to bless each other, as blessing we have known."[24]

While blessings have traditionally been understood as sacred rites by which the Church draws divine favor down upon persons, objects of worship or things of nature, there is a contemporary sense that blessings open us to the sacredness already there resulting from Jesus Christ's sanctification of all persons and things through his paschal mystery, his dying and rising. In acknowledging this sacredness, and Christ as the sanctifier, God is praised and we are blessed. Mary Anthony Wagner, OSB, explains that "though it is God alone who is the source of all blessings for us, in recognizing these gifts we also give voice to God in the blessings, thus participating in them. Anyone who perceives this action of God's redeeming work in faith within creation is in a position to utter that blessing, that praise."[25]

> The Church as the universal sacrament of salvation continues the work of sanctifying and in the Holy Spirit joins Christ its Head in giving glory to the Father.
>
> —*Book of Blessings*, 8

There is a sense in which the prayers in the *Book of Blessings* are oriented toward preparing worshippers to receive the chief effects of the sacraments: "[S]ince they have been established as a kind of imitation of the sacraments, blessings are signs above all of the spiritual effects that are achieved through the Church's intercession."[26] The structure and elements of the blessings found in the *Book of Blessings* constitute an "order" and follow the pattern of the

---

22. BB, 12.
23. *A Book of Blessings*. (Ottawa, Canada: Publications Service, Canadian Conference of Catholic Bishops, 1981), 20.
24. Gregory Norbet, OSB, "That There May Be Bread" which is found on the album, *That There May Be Bread*." Used with permission from the Benedictine Foundation of the State of Vermont.
25. Wagner, 111.
26. BB, 10.

Eucharistic liturgy: a song, Sign of the Cross and greeting; an introduction; an appropriate reading from Scripture, followed by a homily; intercessions; the blessing prayer itself with the minister's hands outstretched (if ordained); and finally, words of dismissal urging those who have celebrated the blessing to go forth renewed in faith. The high point of the ritual of blessing is the Prayer of Blessing spoken by the minister in the name of the believing community, just as the Eucharistic Prayer is the high point of the Mass. In blessings, "as in other sacramental activity, the words of blessing would be empty were they not planted in our hearts and souls first of all, and then overflow into a revelation of God's work within us."[27]

According to performative theory in linguistics, certain words can bring about a state of affairs. For example, when the celebrant says, "Go forth, the Mass is ended," it is over. The prayers in the *Book of Blessings* rest on the ancient principle that as we express our thankful praise to God over people, places, and things, both animate and inanimate, they "are declared to be blessed and blessing both."[28] This is succinctly expressed in the Order for the Blessing of Tools and Other Equipment for Work: "O God, / the fullness of blessing comes down from you, / to you our prayers of blessing rise up."[29] The glorification of God and human sanctification are intertwined in these blessings, and they are "the ends toward which all the Church's other activities are directed."[30]

---

27. BB, 109.

28. Laurence F. X. Brett, *Redeemed Creation: Sacramentals Today, Message of the Sacramentals* (Wilmington, DE: Michael Glazier, 1984), 150–151.

29. BB, 934.

30. BB, 9.

Preparing Parish Blessings

"The source from whom every good gift comes is God,
who is above all, blessed for ever."

—*Book of Blessings*, 1

B lessings are meant to be celebrated regularly by the people of God. They
are a way in which Christians live out their baptismal call to give God
praise and thanksgiving. The act of blessing praises God by proclaiming
his goodness for enabling us to gather in his name and encounter his presence and action in our lives. Blessings acknowledge that God is the source of
every goodness and gift. In very real way, blessings are a means through
which we profess our belief and faith in God and in his goodness.

> Blessings are signs that have God's word as their basis and that are celebrated
> from motives of faith. They are therefore meant to declare and to manifest
> the newness of life in Christ that has its origin and growth in the sacraments
> of the New Covenant established by the Lord. In addition, since they have
> been established as a kind of imitation of the sacraments, blessings are
> signs above all of spiritual effects that are achieved through the Church's
> intercession. . . . the celebration of blessings should truly contribute to
> God's praise and glory and should serve to better God's people.[1]

Blessings implore God's protection. Through these liturgical rites, we
ask God to continue his saving presence and action in our lives and
remember his ancient promises.
Through blessings, we seek God's
mercy. We acknowledge that when all
is said and done, we cannot control
God by our own words or by our ritual

> The celebration of blessings holds a
> privileged place among all the sacramentals
> celebrated by the Church for the pastoral
> benefit of the people of God.
>
> —Decree, *Book of Blessings*
> May 31, 1984

actions—it is only because of his love for us that we are gathered to ask more
from him. In recognizing God's mercy—his unconditional love for us—we
have the courage to ask for his continued presence and action in our lives.

---

1. BB, 10 and 11.

With a blessing, "the Church gives glory to God in all things and is particularly intent on showing forth his glory to those who have been or will be reborn though his grace."[2] Through the celebration of a blessing, the Church specifically asks God to reveal his grace and to be present during particular situations: in pregnancy, in the departure of a parishioner or the arrival of a new one, in the building of a factory or an office, in the use of the Advent wreath, in the meeting of an organization or a group, or in the confines of an elderly person's home. Through a blessing, we ask God to reveal himself as we use religious or secular objects: a rosary, an automobile, seeds that will be planted, the Christmas trees that adorn our homes and sanctuaries, a picture, icon, or stature of a holy person (Jesus, Mary, and the saints). The celebration of these many blessings "are the means for us to profess that as we make use of what God has created we wish to find him and to love and serve him with all fidelity."[3]

The preparation of blessings in the parish would appropriately fall under the responsibilities of the liturgy committee. Blessings are, after all, part of the liturgical life of the parish and are within the scope of the liturgy committee's ministry. Because blessings affect various aspects of the parish, it would be good to invite others who are directly affected by the blessing that is celebrated. For example, if the Order for the Blessing of Catechists is being prepared, the director of religious education might be part of the preparations. Or if the Order for the Blessing a New Building Site is being prepared, some of those connected to the new building may be involved.

The *Book of Blessings*

The blessings of the Church are official rituals and are found in the *Book of Blessings*. The *Book of Blessings* was approved for use in the dioceses of the United States in 1989. It is a translation of the Latin ritual, *De Benedictionibus*. The volume used in the United States also includes forty-two additional orders of blessing[4] that were prepared by the Bishops Committee on Divine Worship.[5] Because of the unique additions prepared by the Conference of Bishops, the *Book of Blessings* will differ from country to country. For example, the

---

2. BB 12.

3. BB, 12.

4. As you review the *Book of Blessings*, you will see "USA" noted in the margins of those blessings that were prepared by the United States bishops.

5. At the time the 1989 *Book of Blessings* was prepared for use in the dioceses of the United States, the committee was called the Committee on the Liturgy of the National Conference of Catholic Bishops.

Bendicional from Mexico, essentially follows the Latin text. The Mexican conference of bishops did add a few blessings, such as the blessing of a flag, the Advent wreath, and the nativity scene, but Mexico did not add as many original blessings as the US bishops

prepared.[6] The Canadian bishops did not prepare a translation of the Latin text. Their edition of *A Book of Blessings* was published in 1981 and included original prayer texts rather than direct translations of the Latin text. It has since gone out of print. Currently, the Canadian Conference of Bishops publishes *Blessings and Prayers for Home and Family*[7] (which is similar to the

Shown here are the individual ritual books for use in the United States, Canada, and Mexico.

United States book, *Catholic Household Blessings and Prayers*) and *Celebrations of Installation and Recognition*. This latter book is similar to the United States *Book of Blessings*, but includes fewer blessings.

The *Book of Blessings* is organized in six main parts with two appendixes. Each part includes orders of blessing that share a common focus or theme, such as those blessings pertaining to persons (part I), buildings and various forms of human activity (part II), objects for use in the church (part III), devotional objects (part IV), feasts and seasons (part V), and various needs and occasions (part VI). For the most part, each blessing is its own chapter, and within that chapter the various forms of the blessing are presented. For example, some blessings

> At all times and in every situation, then, the faithful have an occasion for praising God through Christ in the Holy Spirit, for calling on divine help, and for giving thanks in all things, provided there is nothing that conflicts with the letter and spirit of the Gospel.
>
> —*Book of Blessings*, 13

---

6. At the time of this printing, the Mexican edition is the approved Spanish text for use in the dioceses of the United States. However, a translation approved by the United States bishops is pending confirmation from the Holy See. The promulgation date is unknown as are the publishers of the work. However, the goal with this new Spanish translation was to match the US English edition of the *Book of Blessings*. It is the US bishops' plan that this edition include a third appendix with the blessing of the child of the womb and the blessing on the fifteenth birthday which are currently published as separate supplements in English. The Bishops Committee on Divine Worship (BCDW) will provide updates in their monthly newsletter.

7. This book was also prepared by the Canadian National Liturgy Office and is not a translation of the Latin text.

can be celebrated within Mass or within a celebration of the Word. Usually, a longer and shorter form are provided. Every blessing found in these parts helps the faithful experience God in all persons, in all things, and at all times. The "General Introduction" or praenotanda is found at the beginning of the ritual book and provides a theological and spiritual overview of the meaning and purpose of blessings and well as general guidance for their celebration (such as who may preside and be involved).

Part I

Part I of the *Book of Blessings* includes "Blessings Directly Pertaining to Persons." This includes such blessings as those for families, married couples, baptized children, children who have not yet been baptized, and parents before childbirth. The blessings are not only focused on people, but on particular circumstances of life such as being confined to home or suffering from addiction, crime, and oppressive situations. It is probably the most diverse part of the *Book of Blessings* and includes the greatest number of blessings—twenty-four!

Part II

Part II of the *Book of Blessings* includes, as its title states, those "Blessings Related to Buildings and Various Forms of Human Activity." Here is where you will find blessings of physical structures and specific objects. The buildings for which part II contains blessings range from a new home or building site to a new seminary or religious house; a new school or university to a library or a factory; a parish hall or catechetical center to a gymnasium or athletic field.

The specific situations for which there are blessings in part II all pertain to "human activity." Here there are blessings for various means of transportation (an automobile, train, or motorcycle) as well as blessings for seeds at planting time. There are blessings for things that have to do with work and human labor—tools or technical installations—and things that have to do with play and recreation—boats, fishing gear, and athletic events. One of the most popular orders of blessing used by most parishes in the United States can be found in this part II of the *Book of Blessings*: the blessing of animals, which many parishes celebrate on or near the Feast of St. Francis of Assisi, the patron saint of animals. Many of the blessings found in part II are related to fostering various activities in the lives of humans—sporting activities, the construction of new buildings, the planting and harvesting of crops, and the care of farm animals and pets.

Part III

Part III of the *Book of Blessings* is titled "Blessings of Objects That Are Designed or Erected for Use in Churches, Either in the Liturgy or in Popular Devotions." The Church has long had a history of formally blessing those items or appointments (for example, furniture) that are a standard part of the environment or part of a Catholic church, such as a tabernacle, church doors, bells, or an organ. Part III also includes an order for blessing for an image of a saint, the Blessed Virgin Mary, or Christ as well as the blessing of a chalice, paten, or holy water (this latter blessing takes place outside of Mass). The appointments, or furniture, include a new episcopal chair (or the cathedra of a cathedral) or presidential chair (the chair for the priest celebrant in your own parish), a new ambry (the structure that contains the vessels of holy oils which every parish uses) as well as a baptistry or baptismal font, a new confessional, or Stations of the Cross. It even contains an order for the blessing of a cemetery!

Part IV

Part IV, as its title states, includes "Blessings of Articles Meant to Foster the Devotion of the Christian People." These are blessings that foster the devotional life of the domestic church. Although the objects of blessing in parts III and IV are similar, while part III is concerned with objects for public, liturgical use, part IV is concerned with objects for the private, devotional life of Catholics. Part IV includes a general blessing of religious articles. This would be used for medals, crucifixes, and other images that might be placed in the home, the blessing of rosaries, and the blessing and conferral of the scapular.[8]

---

8. A scapular is a religious garment, and in some religious communities or confraternities it is part of their habit. It is a long rectangular piece of cloth that goes over the head and hangs over the shoulders and down the front and back of a person. So in reality, this blessing is meant for very specific people who are in relationship with a particular religious order or confraternity. The title itself notes that the scapular is being "conferred." This means that the member of the religious community is *receiving* the scapular as part of their habit. Of note here is that many Catholics who are not part of a religious order or confraternity have the devotion of wearing what is also called a "scapular." This form of the scapular is usually two small pieces of cloth bound by two bands. It is worn over the shoulders so that one piece of cloth rests on the chest and the other on the back. This scapular is usually worn under one's clothing and each piece of cloth includes a holy image (such as a saint or the Blessed Virgin Mary) or text (for example, "Holy Passion of Our Lord Jesus Christ save

Part V

Part V of the *Book of Blessings* includes "Blessings Related to Feasts and Seasons." These blessings correspond to the liturgical year and are printed in the order in which you would use them. This section begins with the blessing of the Advent wreath, continues with the seasons and feasts that follow, and concludes with blessings for All Souls' Day and Thanksgiving. The blessings in this section significantly affect the liturgical life of the local Church, since many take place at Mass or involve a sign or symbol that is present at Mass, such as a Christmas tree or nativity scene. These are also blessings and rituals that may be incorporated into the homelife of the domestic Church.

The final blessing in this section might seem initially out of place. Chapter 59 includes the Order for the Blessing of Food or Drink or Other Elements. This blessing may be used at any time during the liturgical year or on particular feasts. Special food and drinks are often a custom that is shared during the seasons and on special feasts, such as hot cross buns on Good Friday, St. Lucia buns on the memorial of St. Lucy (December 13), or wassail (a form of cider) during Christmas. Sometimes it is the custom to bless an object for devotional use on these days, such as placing flowers or candles near an image of the saint who is being honored in the calendar that day. This blessing would be used for all of these purposes.

Part VI

The final part of the *Book of Blessings*, Part VI, includes "Blessings for Various Needs and Occasions." For the most part, these services are used for blessing those involved with the ministerial life of the parish. This includes those who exercise pastoral service (for example a pastoral counselor or a pastoral minister) and liturgical ministers. Blessings are also included for the parish council, parish societies (such as the altar and rosary society or a men's and women's club). The blessings also consider members of the parish community, including blessings such as those for departing and for new parishioners, that stress how vital everyone is for the life of the community.

One blessing found in Part VI does not necessarily have to do with the life of the parish as much as it might have to do with the community in which the parish is located: The Prayer on the Occasion of the Inauguration of a Public

---

us"). The Order of Blessing and Conferral of the Scapular would not be used to bless these devotional scapulars. Instead, one would use the Order for the Blessing of Religious Articles, which is found in chapter 44 of the *Book of Blessings*.

Official. This order might be used, for example, on the inauguration of a new president or mayor. It provides models that can be used as the invocation (prayer to begin the event) and for the benediction (prayer to end the event).

Appendixes

Finally, the *Book of Blessings* includes two appendixes: The Order for the Installation of a Pastor and a collection titled Solemn

The Order for the Blessing of Various Means of Transportation (chapter 21) may be used to bless bicycles.

Blessings and Prayers over the People. The Order for the Installation of a Pastor includes the various forms under which an installation might be celebrated: within Mass or outside Mass, when the bishop is the minister of installation or when a priest is delegated to do such.

The collection of solemn blessings and prayers over the people is for use in various situations and can be used in various ways. For example, these blessings can be used as the conclusion of any of the orders of blessing found in the *Book of Blessings*. They may also be used to conclude celebrations of Morning or Evening Prayer. They could also be used whenever a priest or deacon is asked to give a blessing. Since the *Book of Blessing* specifies that these could be used during Morning or Evening Prayer, it would not be best to use them at Mass.

Blessings as Liturgical Prayer

It is probably more common for blessings to occur very simply—perhaps the presider makes the sign of the cross over the object, place, or person and adds the sprinkling of holy water. He might offer his own spontaneous Prayer of Blessing. There is probably no music, no proclamation of Scripture, and no acclamations for the people to respond. However, orders of blessing are part of the official liturgical prayer of the Church—the public, formal, and communal worship of the gathered Body of Christ. Blessings are a way that the Church honors the mysteries of Christ and marks time. In their liturgical context, blessings are often connected to particular times of the year, both liturgical and secular, and are yet another way for the Church to sanctify time and thank God—from the seeds that will grow into life to the harvest that will feed the hungry; from the breaking of ground to the finished building that will house God's people; and from the new life of a child to the parents that care for them. A blessing, as an official, liturgical act, acknowledges that when the Church gathers in prayer, including the act of blessing, we are, first and foremost, gathering as Christ's Body. As such, united to the One High Priest who is the head of the Body, we do what we were baptized to do: praise God and thank him for his presence in our life. Writing in 1981, Rev. Thomas G. Simons' words still ring true today:

> The priest often functions in the absence of the people, and even if Christians are present, the event often becomes a one-man operation. Often, when the faithful bring objects for blessing, the minister withdraws to the sacristy in order to execute the ritual. Increasingly there should be a working toward more active and conscious participation of the faithful in sacramentals [blessings]. The saying of a short prayer individually, say, even if unavoidable, should be the exception.[9]

> Blessings are a part of the liturgy of the Church. Therefore their communal celebration is in some cases obligatory but in all cases more in accord with the character of liturgical prayer; as the Church's prayer places truth before the minds of the faithful, those who are present are led to join themselves with heart and voice to the voice of the Church.[10]

The "General Introduction" reminds us that "the source from whom every good gift comes is God, who is above all, blessed forever."[11] He is the source of every blessing for which we could ever hope and for which we continually pray. Christ, God's "supreme blessing upon us"[12] is always present, leading us to praise and glorify God. The Holy Spirit helps baptized members of the Church "fulfills its many-sided ministry of sanctifying."[13] In all of this, we continue to do what we were baptized to do: proclaim Christ's glory until he comes again. Blessings, as liturgical prayer, allow us to do that in a variety of wonderful and life-giving ways. Then, "seeking what is pleasing to God, we will fully appreciate his blessing and will surely receive it."[14]

The more that the members of your community experience the celebrations of blessings, the more accustomed the people will become to them as a

---

9. Thomas G. Simons, *Blessings: A Reappraisal of Their Nature, Purpose, and Celebration,* (Saratoga, CA: Resource Publications, 1981), 69.

10. BB, 16.

11. BB, 1.

12. BB, 3.

13. BB, 9.

14. BB, 15.

part of the liturgical life of the parish. The more your parish publicly celebrates blessings, the more the people will come to a deeper understanding of them.

> The liturgical form should awaken he understanding that every liturgical action is a celebration carried on by mutual participation. Those assembled realize that through their presence at a blessing, they need God's grace, that they cannot on their own bring about the healing and perfection of the world.[15]

The frequent celebration of blessings helps the assembly become aware that they are in need of God's grace.

Liturgical Roles and Ministries

The "General Introduction" to the *Book of Blessings* includes a section on the "offices and ministries" of the liturgical celebrations of blessings. Before even addressing the roles of the presider, reader, and other roles (such as musicians and servers), the introduction focuses on the fundamental importance of the presence of the assembly, whether major blessings that concern the local Church (such as the blessing of pastoral ministers) or more simple blessings (such as the blessing of the rosary).

> For the more important blessings that concern the local Church, it is fitting that the diocesan or parish community assembly, with the bishop or pastor (parish priest) presiding, to celebrate the blessing.

> Even in the case of other blessings, the presence of an assembly of the faithful is preferable, since what is done on behalf of any group within the community redounds in some way to the good of the entire community.[16]

When preparing blessings, just as with all liturgies, the "full and active participation by all the people is the aim to be considered before all else."[17] The assembly should be easily drawn into the celebration of blessings through the use of music, good proclamation of Scripture texts, and the dialogical

---

15. Simons, *Blessings*, 69.

16. BB, 16.

17. *Sacrosanctum concilium*, 14.

nature of the prayer texts. Carefully prepared worship aids are a useful tool for helping the assembly take part in a service that might be unfamiliar to them—especially with the unique responses that are found in the various orders of blessing. The assembly will be more engaged with the celebration of blessings if the preparation team regularly incorporates them in the liturgical life of the parish and catechizes about their meaning and importance for our life of faith. Review the table of contents of the *Book of Blessings* in connection with the regular life of the Church—blessings can easily be incorporated whether it's the planning of a parish garden or the blessing of a new staff person. When blessings occur, the assembly should be informed and notified. Use the bulletin and parish social media pages to your advantage. And use the blessing itself as a way to preach about the liturgical rite.

> During the celebration of a blessing and in preaching and catechesis beforehand, priests and ministers should therefore explain to the faithful the meaning and power of blessings. There is further advantage in teaching the people of God the proper meaning of the rites and prayers employed by the Church in imparting blessings.[18]

When preparing blessings, parish teams should still familiarize themselves with key liturgical teachings and norms found in such documents as *Sacrosanctum concilium*, *Sing to the Lord*, and *Built of Living Stones*. The principles used to prepare the Sunday liturgy should guide the celebration of blessings—from music to environment as well as the involvement of liturgical ministers. Because it is liturgical prayer, blessings, especially those affecting the broader local Church, should include a full complement of liturgical ministers: lectors or readers who are able to proclaim the Word of God well; musicians who will lead the gathered assembly in the opening and closing songs; a capable psalmist who can sing the psalm effortlessly while engaging the response of the people; a reader who will announce the intercessions; servers who can assist the presider with the book, the aspergillum, and other

A lay minister blesses an Advent wreath in a Catholic office.

18. BB, 19.

needs; greeters and ministers of hospitality; and those who can appropriately prepare the liturgical space.

Both ordained and lay ministers may preside over a blessing. The "General Introduction" provides the criteria for how this role is determined. It even clarifies the role of bishop, priest, and deacon. First and foremost, "the ministry of blessing involves a particular exercise of the priesthood of Christ and, in keeping with the place and office within the people of God belonging to each person."[19] For example, a lay person may preside over the blessing of a family, parents after a miscarriage, means of transportation, fields and flocks, and even the blessing of throats on the Memorial of St. Blaise. However, there are blessings that are reserved to the ordained—for example, the blessing of a chalice and paten, the blessing of a parish pastoral council, or the blessing of a new episcopal chair. The rubrics will guide preparation teams in determining if lay ministers may preside over the blessing; however, if a priest is present, "the office of presiding should be left to him."[20]

The "General Introduction" states that laypersons who preside "exercise this ministry in virtue of their office (for example, parents on behalf of their children) or by reason of some special liturgical ministry or in fulfillment of a particular charge in the Church."[21] Many parish pastoral ministers are qualified, and their ministry in the parish may include liturgical presiding. In some dioceses pastoral associates or lay ecclesial ministers receive training for presiding.

For any lay minister who presides over a blessings, the presumption is that he or she is trained to do so, just as other liturgical ministers are trained. In some dioceses, especially mission dioceses, the bishop appoints qualified religious (sisters, nuns, monks, and so on) or catechists for presiding at celebrations of blessings. It is best to check with your parish or your local office of worship regarding particular diocesan policy for lay ministers presiding at liturgical rites.

Every liturgical celebration involves primary signs and symbols. The *Book of Blessings* emphasizes that the "outward signs" of blessings are the presider's gestures. "The outward signs or gestures that are especially employed are: the outstretching, raising, or joining of the hands, the laying on of hands,

19. BB, 18.
20. BB, 18.
21. BB, 18.

the sign of the cross, sprinkling with holy water, and incensation."[22] How these signs are celebrated depends upon who is presiding. The rubrics clarify appropriate gestures that are particular to ordained or lay minsters. The orders of blessing include specific directives that take into account the various ministers who may be presiding. For example, as noted before, when it is a priest or deacon who presides, the orders of blessing note that he pronounces the blessing with hands outstretched. When it is a layperson, the Prayer of Blessing is pronounced with hands joined. The use of other gestures and other signs are likewise specifically noted in the directives in terms of who is presiding. Appropriate preparation and planning will help provide what is necessary for a full and rich celebration.

Lay ministers might be curious why "the outstretching, raising, or . . . the laying on of hands" is reserved to the clergy. Recall that the laying on of hands is an expression of priestly ministry, allowing him to act "*in persona Christi capitis*"—as the head of Christ. When the priest presides over a blessing, the act of blessing itself is an extension of the priestly ministry of Christ. Although, we all share in the priestly ministry of Christ through baptism, those actions that are reserved to the clergy reflect the distinction between head of the body and the body at prayer. Likewise to the extension of hands, or the *orans* position. "We are reminded . . . that Jesus himself blessed the disciples at the ascension with extended hands. He took children into his arms and blessed them, laying his hands upon them."[23] By virtue of his ordination, outside of Mass a deacon may also assume these gestures, as is indicated by other rituals, such as *Sunday Celebrations in the Absence of a Priest* and *Holy Communion and Worship of the Eucharist outside Mass*.

When presiding over a blessing at Mass, priests and assisting deacons should wear proper vesture: an alb, a stole, and a chasuble or dalmatic in the color of the day. If presiding over a blessing outside of Mass—whether in church or in another location—priests and deacons may wear their alb and stole. A cope may also be worn. The cope and stole should be white or the color of the day. If the presider is wearing a cassock, he may wear the surplice instead of the alb. In more formal blessings, a lay man or woman would wear an alb (if presiding at family functions in the home, the alb is not necessary).

22. BB, 26.
23. Simons, *Blessings*, 69.

A bishop should consult the *Ceremonial of Bishops* for the proper vestments to wear.[24]

The preparation team should ensure that presiders and liturgical ministers use the proper liturgical books when serving during the blessing: multiple copies of the *Book of Blessings* should be readily available for presiders and readers. It is not likely that the *Lectionary for Mass* would be used, although parish teams may certainly select alternate readings from that ritual text. Provide the team with access to a Bible. The *Book of Blessings* includes many options for Scripture to be proclaimed in which these passages do not appear in full in either the lectionary or the *Book of Blessings* itself. A Bible will be needed to access these text. Ritual binders may be prepared for individual ministers to avoid using printouts and sheets of paper during all forms of prayer.

Lay ministers join their hands or continue to hold the book or ritual binder while blessing.

Liturgical Order of Prayer

Each blessing follows a particular format or "order" of prayer. This includes Introductory Rites, the proclamation of Scripture, the singing of hymns and psalms, dialogical prayers, and formal Prayers of Blessing—even a homily. The gathered assembly offers intercessions for the world and may offer the Lord's Prayer. The orders of blessing end with a Closing Rite that is similar to other liturgies of the Church—a general blessing and a dismissal of some form. Blessings are a liturgical act, a ritual celebration.

Those who prepare blessings in the parish should look at the rubrics very carefully. Each blessing is preceded by introductory material stating the purpose of the blessing and offering details for its celebration, including suggestions for when the blessing might take place during the year. For example, the introductory material for the Order for the Blessing of Rosaries (chapter

---

24. The liturgies of blessing are found in Part VI (Sacramentals) of the *Ceremonial of Bishops*.

45) suggests that the ritual take place on "feasts or memorials of Mary or on the occasion of a pilgrimage."[25]

Each blessing is unique, and assumptions shouldn't be made about its proper celebration—even the sprinkling of holy water, a common practice, is not always called for. The rubrics will indicate whether the blessing may take place during Mass or as its own rite, usually within a Liturgy of the Word. When a blessing takes place within the Mass, the *Book of Blessings* gives direction for which part of the Mass the blessing should take place in and how it should be celebrated. For example, some blessings take place after the homily, while others are celebrated after the prayer after Communion. Another example is that when the blessing of the Advent wreath (chapter 47) takes place during Mass, the blessing occurs after the universal prayer (sample intercessions are even provided in the *Book of Blessings*). Likewise, if it takes place during Mass, the blessing of mothers on Mother's Day (which takes the form of a prayer over the people, chapter 55) replaces the solemn blessing of the day.

The orders of blessing also include shorter forms of the rite. The short forms are intended to be used for particular circumstances. The *Book of Blessings* will advise you of best practice. For example, the longer form for the Order for the Blessing of Rosaries (chapter 45) takes place outside of Mass and is meant to be used when a large number of rosaries are being blessed. This is stated in the introductory material that precedes the ritual text.[26] For situations in which a single rosary is to be blessed, the introductory material recommends that the shorter rite is used. Similarly, the Order for the Blessing of Travelers (chapter 9) includes a shorter rite, "if just one traveler is to be blessed or a small group."[27] For example, the shorter rite might be used may be when one person in the parish is traveling for work and seeks a blessing from the pastor, or if a family in the parish is traveling a long distance.

Parish liturgy teams should also take note that in some cases, such as with the blessing of mothers (chapter 55) and fathers (chapter 56), only one option is provided in its shorter form. In these cases, the introductory material indicates that the blessing is to take place during Mass, but the short form of the rite provides intercessions that are added to the regular universal prayer, and a prayer over the people which is to replace the usual solemn blessing.

---

25. BB, 1464.
26. See BB, 1463.
27. BB, 619.

Blessings within a Liturgy of the Word

The most common way to celebrate a blessing is within a Liturgy of the Word, rather than during Mass. "The typical celebration of a blessing consists of two parts: first, the proclamation of the word of God, and second, the praise of God's goodness and the petition for his help."[28] Each blessing also includes short Introductory and Concluding Rites.

Introductory Rites

Preparation teams should consult the rubrics carefully when preparing the Introductory Rites. For example, some blessings indicate the inclusion of an entrance procession with crossbearer, a reader or deacon carrying the *Book of the Gospels*, and an opening song. Although even if an opening song is not called for, it would be appropriate to include a song or hymn to open the celebration. As a liturgical act, singing serves to unify the individuals who have gathered into one body, one community. This ritual element should not be skipped over lightly. Even if instrumental accompaniment is not available, every effort should be made to begin with a familiar hymn or song that can help situate the celebration in the liturgical life of the Church.

Most of the major Catholic music publishers of the United States now include a topical index. This is an ordering of the music in the hymnal according to topics or themes. For example, the topic of "Reconciliation" is given, and then all the songs or hymns that are in that hymnal and have the theme of reconciliation are listed. This feature is most helpful in considering songs and hymns for use in orders of blessing. For example, for the blessing of animals, look under "Creation," or "Praise." For the blessing of an Advent wreath, look under "Advent," or "Light," since light is such a prominent symbol with the Advent wreath.

Typically, a blessing will begin with the sign of the cross, and every blessing includes a greeting and a response. Particular texts and gestures are provided for ordained presiders and lay ministers (if a lay minister may preside). If the presider is ordained, the people's response is simple, "And with your spirit." Because the *Book of Blessings* has yet to be retranslated, the responses that are printed in the ritual text is the former, "And also with

---

28. BB, 20.

you."[29] The responses from the third edition of *The Roman Missal* supersede those in the *Book of Blessings* and should be used.[30] However, the texts that are provided for lay minister will introduce the assembly to unfamiliar responses—the responses will vary from blessing to blessing. For example, in the Order of Blessing a Victim of Crime or Oppression, the lay minister greets the faithful with "May the Lord grant us peace, now and for ever." The assembly responds, "Amen." Whereas in the Order for the Blessing of Elderly People Confined to their Homes, the assembly responds to the lay presider's greeting with "Blessed be God now and for ever" or "Amen." Consider the assembly's needs. How will they know how to respond? Worship aids will be very helpful.

Unlike other celebrations of the Word, there most often is no collect. Most often the ritual provides an introduction that explains the nature of the blessing and prepares the assembly for what is about to occur. The presider may use the text that is provided in the ritual or write his or her own text. Even if one decides to compose his or her own remarks to introduce the blessing, it is always best to start with what the Church has already given us. Powerful images and phrases can be found in these introductory remarks and serve as a wonderful starting point for catechizing the faithful.

The Proclamation of the Word of God

After the Introductory Rites, the order of blessing calls for the proclamation of the Word. Since the Second Vatican Council, the proclamation of the Word has regained a central spot in the liturgical rites. *Sacrosanctum concilium*, which decreed the liturgical revisions that should take place following the Council, stated:

> Sacred Scripture is of the greatest importance in the celebration of the liturgy. For it is from Scripture that the readings are given and explained in the homily and that psalms are sung; the prayers, collects, and liturgical songs

---

29. A lay minister should not use those texts that are proper to the ordained. The texts that a bishop, priest, or deacon use point their liturgical role as head of the Church and head of the assembly as standing in *persona Christi capitis*. As Paul Turner writes: [The greeting and its response, "And with your spirit"] "express a desire that the Lord be present to the spirit of the entire community. Based on evidence from Paul's letters, the priest's line could imply, "The Lord be with your spirit," and the people's line would then reciprocate: "and with *your* spirit." . . . the dialogue establishes the interdependence of the priest [and deacon] and the people as they take up their roles to praise God" (*Understanding the Revised Mass Texts*, 8–9).

30. Likewise, when praying the prayers of blessing, the endings provided in the *Book of Blessings* ("We ask this through" or "Grant this through") should be changed to what is in the missal, a simple, "Through Christ our Lord."

are scriptural in their inspiration; it is from the Scriptures that actions and signs derive their meaning.[31]

Every order of blessing includes the proclamation of Scripture.

"The Word of God calls us to follow. God speaks to us before we pray or respond. Our relationship does not begin with us speaking to God. It starts when God speaks."[32] Whenever we gather for liturgical celebrations and the Word is proclaimed, we hear a portion of the story of salvation history. Thus the context of God's saving actions in the course of human history is what surrounds every celebration of a blessing. Even the blessing itself is the next instance of God's saving presence and action in the lives of those who have gathered.

Paragraph 29 of the *General Instruction of the Roman Missal* states: "When the Sacred Scriptures are read in the Church, God himself speaks to his people." This is liturgical principle holds true for *any* liturgy of the Church, and not only the Mass. The Scriptures that are proclaimed during an order of blessing are the living Word of God, and as such they demand a response from thosewho have gathered as the Body of Christ. Paul Turner writes:

> Our Christian lives begin with and thrive on the Word of God and that we believe that Word has power. Engaging that Word is the privilege and task of every Christian. God's Word called us into discipleship. God's Word guides us throughout discipleship. The more we open our ears, the more the Scripture warms our heart and refreshes our perspective on life.

When a blessing takes place as its own ritual (that is, outside of Mass), a short reading is proclaimed first, which is followed by the singing of a psalm. The ritual text provides a suggested text as well as additional options. For example, in the Order for the Blessing of a New Religious House (chapter 13), the ritual suggests the proclamation of Hebrews 13:1–2, 5–7, 14–17 or John 1:35–42. It also provides the option of looking to the texts provided in the *Lectionary for Mass* in Masses for Various Needs and Occasions (For Religious) or the ritual Mass for the Consecration to a Life of Virginity and Religious

---

31. *Sacrosanctum concilium*, 24

32. Paul Turner, *Guide for Lectors and Readers*, 2nd ed. (Chicago: Liturgy Training Publications, 2021), 6.

Profession. Although the order of service suggests that only one reading be proclaimed followed by the psalm, parish preparation teams may add other readings. If a Gospel is chosen, it "always holds the place of honor."[33] It should be noted that the *Book of Blessings* does not require that only a priest or deacon proclaim the Gospel. A lay minister may be chosen to do so. Having a Bible handy will be helpful for ministers when proclaiming a text that is not provided in the liturgical books.

Careful preparation will include a review of all the options given so as to ascertain which reading is better suited to the specific celebration, to those who have gathered, or to the liturgical season in which the blessing is celebrated. Just as at Mass, be sure to incorporate moments of silence between readings and the psalm. Parish readers and presiders should take note that the invitation to the readings varies from what is used at Mass. Rather than introducing the reading as we do at Mass (that is, "A reading from the Book of the Prophet Isaiah"), the readings at a blessing are introduced with "Brothers and sisters, listen to the words of the Book of the Prophet Isaiah." It is a more active introduction that calls the assembly to *do* something—that is, to listen. The readings should of course take place at the ambo. Note that even if a Gospel is prescribed (for example in the blessing of a new religious house), the formulas and ritual actions from Mass are not used. The usual dialogue that precedes the reading of the Gospel is not used—there is no procession, no acclamation, no signing of the forehead, lips, and heart. The minister simply begins the reading of the Gospel with "Brothers and sisters, listen to the words of the holy gospel according to [St.] John."

It is best that the responsorial psalm be sung, just as at Mass. The psalm "is an integral part of the Liturgy of the Word and which has great liturgical and pastoral importance, since it fosters meditation on the Word of God."[34] Use settings that are familiar to the assembly and provide the antiphon in a worship aid. A cantor will be needed for its proclamation.

> Because of the great importance of the psalm in the Liturgy of the Word, the psalm is normally sung from the ambo (or other appropriate place). The cantor intones the response, which the assembly repeats back. The

---

33. BB, 712.
34. GIRM, 61.

cantor then proclaims the verses to the psalm, and the people respond to what they have heard by singing their response after each verse.[35]

The homily or explanation of the reading (if a lay person presides) follows the readings.

In many instances the orders of blessing provide particular intercessions that may be used in their entirety, adapted, or added to texts prepared by the parish liturgy team. The ritual text usually provides a particular response that differs from the usual "Lord, hear our prayer." If using the response found in the ritual text, again, the assembly will need to be made aware of the response so that they can participate fully. The intercessions should be offered by the deacon, if he is present, or a reader may fulfill this role. A cantor may also chant the intercessions and lead the assembly with a musical response. Use settings that are familiar to the assembly.

In some cases, the intercessions are followed by the communal praying of the Lord's Prayer, and then the Prayer of Blessing takes place. However, in most cases the Prayer of Blessing itself concludes the intercessions.

The Prayer of Blessing

The blessing itself may vary among the orders contained in the *Book of Blessings*. However, all of them contain some central, common elements. Each blessing is made up of a specific, formal prayer that may be accompanied by a ritual act—the sprinkling of holy water, the use of incense, the laying on of hands.

The presence and participation of the assembly and liturgical ministers stresses the importance of blessings for the life of the parish community.

The Prayer of Blessing follows a familiar pattern. First, God is praised for some action or for some specific deed he has done in our history that is connected to the blessing being celebrated. The prayer given in the blessing of a Christmas tree, for example (part V, chapter 49), recalls the imagery of light that has been used throughout our tradition when speaking of God's presence to his people. This prayer continues by

35. Jennifer Kerr Budziak, *Guide for Cantors*, 3rd ed. (Chicago: Liturgy Training Publications, 2021), 23.

praising God for his presence here, now, at this moment—symbolized by the lights of the tree now being blessed.

From there, the Prayer of Blessing asks God for his action or his presence in this specific situation. It asks God to continue doing what the Scriptures and our tradition have always proclaimed him as doing: being present to us his people, saving us, bringing us through challenges and struggles, redeeming us through Christ Jesus. The "General Introduction" notes that God's blessings have always been "a promise of divine help, a proclamation of his favor, a reassurance of his faithfulness to the covenant he had made with his people."[36]

Within some orders of blessing, the prayer is accompanied by some ritual act or ritual gesture. These acts or gestures "are in themselves forms of preaching the Gospel and of expressing faith.[37] Depending on the blessing and who is presiding, the order may call for the presider to pray the blessing with outstretched hands or with hands joined or with hands raised. For example, when the presider is an ordained minister, he prays the Prayer of Blessing with hands outstretched. If the presider is a layperson, he or she prays the prayer with hands joined.

The order may call for the tracing of the sign of the cross, which is "an ancient tradition."[38] In 2002, the Congregation for Divine Worship and the Discipline of the Sacraments did clarify the use of the sign of the cross. There is an inconsistency in the texts, and although some orders of blessing do not specify use of the cross, it should be done.[39] Some of the orders provide for the sprinkling of holy water, which in addition to the blessing taking place always calls us to remember the paschal mystery of Christ and our baptismal faith. Finally, some orders call for the use of incense, which is a sign of veneration and honor.

The guidelines and directives of each order notes the specific circumstances in which any of these ritual acts may be used and who can use them. As always, careful preparation will help prepare what would be needed for any specific blessing.

---

36. BB, 6.

37. BB, 27.

38. BB, 26C.

39. See the Latin text, Congregation for Divine Worship and the Discipline of the Sacraments, Prot. N. 1745/02/L (14 September 2002), AAS 94 (2002) 684.

Concluding Rites

Blessings conclude with familiar elements: a dismissal, sign of the cross, and a closing song. Texts are provided for ordained and lay ministers, and these ministers should use the appropriate gestures assigned to their role. An ordained minister will make the

Because some blessings have a special relationship to the sacraments, they may sometimes be joined with the celebration of Mass.

—*Book of Blessings*, 28

sign of the cross over the assembly, whereas a lay minister will make the sign of the cross on himself or herself. When selecting a closing song, consider songs of praise or those that express the faith of the Church and the particular blessing that has been celebrated.

Blessings during Mass

As you review the table of contents of the *Book of Blessings*, you will see that several orders of blessing include a separate service for the blessing to take place within Mass, blessings such as those for families, wedding anniversaries, missionaries, the Advent wreath, the Christmas tree, and throats. Most of these blessings are those that affect the broader local Church community: "blessings are intended, first of all, for the faithful."[40] Some blessings are specifically prohibited from being celebrated during Mass. For example, the blessing of an image of Christ, the Blessed Virgin, or a saint, specifically notes that "the rite is not to be celebrated within Mass."[41]

When deciding whether a blessing can or should take place during Mass or as a separate service as a Liturgy of the Word, the guiding principle should be the worshipping community. In which context will more of the local Church be able to participate fully and experience and be formed by the blessing and the liturgical year? More often than not, it is more appropriate to celebrate these orders during Mass. When the blessing takes place, the assembly should be able to see and actively participate in the order.

The orders of service for a blessing during Mass are quite simple and straightforward. The ritual text presupposes that the Mass take place as usual with the blessing itself taking place following the universal prayer or during the Concluding Rite. Pay particular attention to the rubrics surrounding the

40. BB, 31.
41. BB, 1259.

homily; if a blessing follows the universal prayer, the rubrics do seem to indicate that the Creed be omitted. If the blessing takes place after the universal prayer, the Prayer of Blessing replaces the usual concluding prayer. The *Book of Blessings* often provides a complete set of intercessions for use during the universal prayer, or additional petitions that may be added to those the parish has already prepared—for example, for the blessing of the Advent wreath. In other blessings, such as those for Mother's and Father's Day, the blessing takes place in the form of a prayer over the people, and it replaces the regular

A couple celebrates their wedding anniversary at Mass with a blessing.

blessing or prayer over the people from the missal. In most instances at Mass, the blessing itself is the prayer during which the presider holds his hands outstretched over the persons or things that are to be blessed. Some blessings include the sprinkling with holy water or incensing (for example, the blessing of new church doors includes the sprinkling with holy water; the blessing of a new episcopal or presidential chair includes incensing). In these cases, the sprinkling or incensing most often follows the Prayer of Blessing itself. As mentioned earlier, the proper minister for a blessing at Mass is the priest celebrant. If a deacon is present, he may assist the priest. Vestments of the day are worn.

The *Book of Blessings* does specify which blessings may be celebrated at Mass and "no blessings expect those so specified may be joined with the eucharistic celebration."[42] It may be tempting to want to add a blessing at Mass, such as the blessing of new rosaries or a new image of Mary, but unless the rubrics specify, it may not be done.

When a blessing of people is being celebrated (such as the blessing of students and teachers) the positioning of those being blessed can happen in a number of different ways. If the group of people is small, and can comfortably gather in front of the sanctuary, they can be invited to come forward. In this case, they can stand facing the presider, who is in the sanctuary. However, if they are invited forward and then turn around to face the people, their faces can easily be seen by the congregation. In this case the presider

---

42. BB, 28.

would simply move into the center aisle and face those being blessed. If the number of people being blessed is large, calling them forward may not be possible. In this case, they may be invited to stand at their place. This is the manner often used, for example, for the blessing of mothers on Mother's Day, when there most likely would be a large number of women who would be blessed.

There are a good number of reasons why a parish might choose to celebrate a blessing at Sunday Mass, when this option is provided in the *Book of Blessings*. The Sunday Mass is the preeminent gathering of the Body of Christ in any parish, and thus to celebrate an appropriate blessing ensures the fullest participation of the faithful. For example, the blessing of students and teachers at the beginning of the school year is a most appropriate addition to the Sunday Mass. Every parish has students of every age and level of education, including adults (for example, those in ongoing adult faith formation and those involved with the Christian initiation of adults). The vast majority of parishes will have at least a few teachers and catechists. The education of our children and those who facilitate it are vital to any community, and celebrating this blessing with them at Mass is a profound expression of God's care and concern for them, but the parish's as well. In this section, we will explore some of the blessings that may be celebrated during Mass.

The Blessing of the Advent Wreath during Mass

The blessing of the Advent wreath is found in chapter 47 of the *Book of Blessings*. It may take place during a service of the Word, Evening Prayer, or at Mass. What follows is an explanation of how this blessing may take place during Mass.

Although it originated as a devotion of the domestic Church, the Advent wreath has become a seasonal staple in just about every parish church. As a means of helping mark the passing of the season, it is a sign of the hopeful expectation that is at the heart of Advent. It is quite fitting then that the community should gather, as the season begins, to bless the wreath.

Traditionally, the Advent wreath is a circle of evergreens that may be accentuated with flowers and branches. The greens and flowers should not be fake, for "the use of living flowers and plants, rather than artificial greens, serves as a reminder of the gift of life God has given to the human community."[43] It is common for the four candles to be three violet and one rose (which is

---

43. *Built of Living Stones* (BLS), 129.

lighted on Gaudete Sunday), although the rubrics indicate that four violet and four white candles may be used as well. There is no white "Christ-candle" in the center. *Built of Living Stones* recommends that "objects such as the Advent wreath, the Christmas crib, and other traditional seasonal appointments proportioned to the size of the space and to the other furnishings can enhance the prayer and understanding of the parish community."[44] The rubrics also note that "it may be suspended from the ceiling or placed on a stand."[45] Although the wreath is allowed to be placed in the sanctuary, it should not interfere with the ritual actions of Word and sacrament (specifically, it should not "obscure the altar, lectern, or chair"[46]).

When the blessing occurs at Mass, the rubrics direct that it be the first Mass of the season. For most parishes, this will be the Saturday evening vigil Mass for the first Sunday of Advent. The priest celebrant presides over the blessing (however, if the blessing takes place outside of Mass, a deacon or lay minister may preside). The vestments of the day are worn. Mass takes place as usual, with the blessing itself taking place after the universal prayer. The Prayer of Blessing serves as the concluding prayer to the universal prayer. *The Book of Blessings* includes intercessions that may be used and that can be adapted for the specific needs of the parish. Consider using these intercessions, as their imagery captures so much that is at the heart of the Advent season. It makes sense that some of these would be included among the petitions prepared for this weekend. An introduction to the universal prayer is also provided. After the Prayer of Blessing, the first candle on the wreath is lit, and the Mass continues with the preparation of the gifts.

The Advent wreath is only blessed once; the candles are lit at subsequent liturgies.

The order of blessing gives no indication about who lights the candle. In its simplest form, the presider, after praying the Prayer of Blessing, might light the candle. An acolyte or server might come forward after the blessing to light the candle. However, consider this an opportunity to involve more people of the parish. Individual parishioners could be invited on the first

44. BLS, 128.
45. BB, 1512.
46. BB, 1512.

Sunday when the wreath is blessed, and on the following Sundays, to be the one to light the candles of the wreath (which will take place prior to the collect).

The rubrics indicate that the homily of the day should explain the meaning of the blessing. This can easily be done in some introductory comments at the end of the homily, before the introduction to the universal prayer (general intercessions). The rubrics seem to indicate that the creed be omitted, as it directs that the petitions of the universal prayer directly follow the homily.[47]

Once the intercessions are announced by a deacon, reader, or cantor, the priest offers the Prayer of Blessing. The *Book of Blessings* provides two options. The first option speaks of the Church waiting for the one who "enlightens our hearts and dispels the darkness of ignorance and sin.[48] The second one references Christ as "Emmanuel, the hope of the peoples . . . the wisdom that teaches and guides us . . . the Savior of every nation."[49] Both options end by asking God to bless *us* (rather than the wreath itself), the gathered assembly, "as we light the candles of this wreath." The priest extends his hands over the wreath. There is no sprinkling with holy water or incensation. After the Prayer of Blessing the first candle is lighted by either the presider or someone else, and the Mass continues with the preparation of the gifts and the altar.

The rubrics are quite clear that the wreath is blessed only once: either before or at the first Mass of the season.[50] It is not appropriate to repeat the blessing at each Mass. In fact, for every Mass that follows, the candles of the wreath are lit before Mass begins or immediately before the collect; no further rites or prayers take place.[51]

If the candles are lit before the collect, this should be done most simply. In other words, whoever is to light the candle should do so with no accompanying words or invitation, as the rubric notes. He or she (or a family) comes forward silently with a lit taper, lights the candles, and then the presider follows immediately with the collect. Such simple and dignified actions most appropriately reflect the theology and spirituality of the season of Advent.

---

47. See BB, 1517 and 1518.
48. See BB, 1519.
49. BB, 1520.
50. See BB, 1509 and 1513.
51. See BB, 1513.

The Blessing of Students and Teachers during Mass

The blessing of students and teachers is found in chapter 5 of the *Book of Blessings*. It may take place in a service of the Word or during Sunday Mass. Although this order of blessing includes the blessing of teachers and students at the same time, it may be adapted so that these blessings take place at separate times.[52]

Bless teachers, catechists, and students before school begins, during Catholic Schools Week, or on Catechetical Sunday.

It is appropriate to celebrate this blessing the Sunday before school starts in the local community, on Catechetical Sunday (which always falls on the third Sunday of September), or for Catholic Schools Week (the last week of January). Prepare the blessing for one Mass on a particular Sunday, and advertise it well ahead of time, inviting all teachers, students who live in the parish, and their families.

Mass follows as usual with the blessing, following the universal prayer. The rubrics seem to suggest that the creed be omitted.[53] The rubrics direct that the homily should make note of the blessing and explain the meaning of the celebration.[54] The priest celebrant offers the blessing at Mass, although if the blessing takes place outside of Mass, a deacon or lay minister may preside. The vestments of the day are worn.

The order of blessing provides four petitions, specifically mentioning the students, teachers, and even parents of the students. It is appropriate to add these intercessions to those regularly prepared for the Sunday Mass. The order of service includes the regular response "Lord, hear our prayer" as well as "Fill us with your wisdom, Lord." If using the alternative option, the assembly will need to have the text in order to respond.

The Prayer of Blessing for students and teachers takes the place of the concluding prayer of the universal prayer. The rubrics do not recommend where the students and teachers should be located during the blessing. Since the assembly will already be standing for the universal prayer, it would make

---

52. See BB, 523.
53. See BB, 526 and 527.
54. See BB, 526.

good pastoral sense for the presider to invite the students and teachers to come forward after the homily and stand in front of the altar.

After the conclusion of the petitions, the priest extends his hands over the students and teachers who have gathered before him and offers the Prayer of Blessing. The order provides two options for the prayer. The first asks God to bless both students and teachers together, asking God to "send your Spirit upon these students and teachers / and fill them with your wisdom and blessing."[55] The second includes an invocation for the students first, asking that they "enjoy their learning / and take delight in new discoveries."[56] The prayer then asks that the teachers "strive to share their knowledge with gentle patience and endeavor always to bring the truth to eager minds." After the blessing, the students and teachers are invited to return to their places (there is no sprinkling or incensing), and the Mass continues with the preparation of the gifts and the altar.

Order for the Blessing of a New Tabernacle

The blessing of a new tabernacle is found in chapter 33, part III. Although this may be obvious, the rubrics note that "the most fitting manner"[57] for the celebration of this blessing is a blessing during Mass. It also notes that if the rubrics permit, the Mass and readings be for the votive Mass for the Holy Eucharist. This is an appropriate option if the votive Mass is allowed. Since this is the blessing of one of the most prominent appointments of any parish church, it seems even *more* appropriate that it be celebrated during one of the Sunday Masses, when the most number of parishioners can be present. If the Mass is on a day when votive Masses are not allowed, then the Mass and readings of the day are used.

> The tabernacle or eucharistic reservation is a reminder of Christ's presence that comes about in the sacrifice of the Mass. But it is also a reminder of the brothers and sisters we must cherish in charity.
> —*Book of Blessings*, 1192

Although the blessing of a new tabernacle may take place on any Sunday of the year, determining exactly when to schedule the blessing will depend on a couple of considerations. When the parish needs to begin using the

---

55. BB, 528.
56. BB, 529.
57. BB, 1193.

tabernacle should be the top consideration. After this, give consideration to the liturgical season or the theme of the readings and orations of any given Sunday. For example, if the need is not immediate, it might be better to wait for Easter Time rather than celebrate the blessing during Lent. Obviously, any Sunday with a focused theme of the Eucharist would be especially appropriate—for example, the Solemnity of the Most Holy Body and Blood of Christ, or the six Sundays of the Bread of Life Discourse in Year B.

In general, the Mass proceeds as usual. If ritual Masses are allowed, such as on a Sunday in Ordinary Time, the readings and prayers may be from the Votive Mass for the Holy Eucharist. As with all blessings, the homilist is encouraged to reflect on the meaning of the blessing. However, this blessing is unique. Unlike other blessings, this order of blessing does not include petitions for the universal prayer. Parish teams should prepare those texts as usual and consider including those that involve the eucharistic life of parish (including participation at Mass, devotion to the Eucharist, the sick, and missionary discipleship). Following the universal prayer, the priest celebrant goes to the new tabernacle and invites the assembly, who is still standing, to pray with "Let us pray." As with the collect at the beginning of Mass, this is a call to silent prayer. Give the assembly time to do just that. The priest proceeds with the Prayer of Blessing with his hands outstretched over the tabernacle. The Prayer of Blessing asks that God "bless us and the tabernacle we have prepared / for the sacrament of Christ's body and blood."[58] The priest then places incense in the thurible and incenses the tabernacle. After the Prayer of Blessing, the tabernacle is incensed. Recall that incense is a sign of honor and is most appropriate given the prominence of the tabernacle among our liturgical appointments. The censor or thurible should be accessible to the server who will be carrying it, and the coals should be lit at an appropriate time so they are burning already when the incense is placed on them (for example, toward the end of the homily).

The Mass continues with the preparation of the gifts and altar. After all have received Communion, the ciborium or pyx containing the remaining Eucharist is placed on the altar. The priest prays the prayer after Communion, and a procession to the newly blessed tabernacle forms so that the consecrated hosts may be placed inside. This might include the thurifer, with incense and thurible, followed by two candle-bearers, the deacon if one is assisting at this Mass, and then the priest, with a humeral veil, carrying the ciborium. (Note:

---

58. BB, 1194.

while the order of blessing does not mention the humeral veil, it is being suggested here given its presence in other liturgical rites that include a procession with the blessed sacrament.) During the procession, an antiphon or psalm may be sung—the *Book of Blessings* suggests Psalm 34 with the antiphon "Taste and see the goodness of the Lord," or *"Ave, verum Corpus."* Select settings that are familiar to the assembly.

Once the procession reaches the new tabernacle, the priest places the ciborium in it and leaves the door open. He then places incense in the thurible and incenses the Blessed Sacrament. After a "suitable pause for to pray in silence," he closes the tabernacle door and offers the final blessing.[59] A solemn blessing is provided in the order of blessing. The text asks God to "bless us and make us holy / through Christ's death and resurrection, / [that] Christ . . . / who is present here, invisible in the sacrament of the altar, / . . . bring us the grace that comes from his sacrifice alone, / . . . [and that] for all who come here to consider prayerfully / the work of their salvation . . . / the Lord present in the Eucharist be an inexhaustible fountain of living water."[60] The other option is a prayer over the people in which we ask the Lord that we be "led to a more fruitful sharing / in the memorial of our redemption."[61]

If there is no procession—for example, if the new tabernacle is located directly behind the altar, against the back wall—the priest goes to the tabernacle with the ciborium. A server, with thurible and incense, accompanies him. The priest kneels and then incenses the Blessed Sacrament. After all have prayed in silence, the priest closes the door of the tabernacle. He then prays the solemn blessing or prayer over the people and dismisses the people in the usual way. If it is the custom, the closing song is sung and the ministers process out.

Blessings Celebrated outside of Mass inside or outside of the Church

Many blessings may be celebrated outside of the church proper and may take place within a celebration of the Word (such as the blessing of animals, or the blessing of fields and flocks). Blessings outside of church are not "lesser" celebrations because they take place outside of Mass. We need to do all we can to form our people and to shape our parishes' liturgical life in regard to the

---

59. BB, 1197.
60. BB, 1198.
61. BB, 1199.

celebration of blessings (such as by frequent celebrations of blessings and catechetical bulletin inserts about blessings). Blessings outside of church are still liturgical rites that contribute to a fuller expression of the community's faith.

When celebrating blessings outside of the church, they should be prepared as carefully as those celebrated within Mass. There should be a full complement of ministers: cross bearer, servers, trained readers or lectors, music ministers, greeters, and ushers. If at all possible, music should be part of the celebration.

Order for the Blessing of Animals

The Order for the Blessing of Animals is found in chapter 25. This blessing is often celebrated on or around the Memorial of St. Francis of Assisi, the patron saint of animals, on October 4. This well-loved celebration for both Catholic and Protestant communities is often advertised as the blessing of pets. It is a wonderful celebration in which parishioners are invited to gather at the church and bring their beloved animals in order to ask God's blessing on these important members of our families—cats and dogs, birds and fish, ferrets, bunnies, and hamsters; all creatures of our God and king! So to prevent any discord among the animals, pet guardians should be advised to bring their pets on leashes and harnesses or in carriers.

> Just as happens when we fall in love with someone, whenever [Francis] would gaze at the sun, the moon or the smallest of animals, he burst into song, drawing all other creatures into his praise. He communed with all creation. . . .
>
> —*Laudato Si'*, 11

Presuming that this blessing is not celebrated in the church (although this is most certainly an option), consider gathering people in front of the Church or at another part of the parish property—for example, a plaza, parish garden, or an open area of yard. Although this blessing normally takes place at parish churches for our domestic pets, it can most certainly be used at farms, zoos, and animal shelters. When blessings take place outside, you will need to consider the visual and auditory needs of the assembly. Can they see the ritual action and easily take part? Are they able to hear the ministers? Are microphones and speakers set up? You may also need to set up a lectern to serve as the ambo.

The blessing of animals does not take place in Mass; the order of service is a celebration of the Word of God, or Liturgy of the Word. Its format includes the Introductory Rites, a Reading of the Word of God with a homily or reflection, intercessions, the Prayer of Blessing, and the Concluding Rite. A full complement of liturgical ministers should be scheduled for the celebration: greeters or ushers to help the people and pets assemble, servers to assist the minister, music ministers, and trained parish readers. A worship aid should be provided to help the assembly participate. A priest, deacon, or lay minister may serve as presider. The lay minister should use those texts and gestures prescribed for him or her. A priest or deacon should be vested in an alb and stole, or cassock and surplice—even a cope may be worn. A lay minister should wear an alb. The minister might chose to "adapt the celebration to the circumstances of the place and the people involved"; however, the "structure and chief elements of the rite" should be maintained.[62] For example, if there is a large number of animals and a prolonged period of time is a concern with so many, the psalm after the reading, or the intercessions, may be omitted.

At the scheduled time, the ministers and the people with their pets gather, and an opening song may be sung. This is most appropriate and, if at all possible, should be included. The cantor, accompanied by a portable instrument—flute, guitar, electronic keyboard—could easily help lead the assembly in singing hymns such as "All Creatures of Our God and King" or "Canticle of the Sun." If instrumentation can't be provided, consider beginning the celebration with the a cappella singing of a well-known song, such as "Praise God from Whom All Blessings Flow."

The blessing of animals reminds us that God has "given us care over living things" (BB, 958).

After the opening song, the presider begins with the sign of the cross and greeting. The order provides a substantial introduction that prepares the assembly to celebrate the blessing. Although the presider may offer his or her own introduction using similar words, consider using what is provided in the ritual text. It expounds upon the beautiful theology of God's creation and that animals "share in Christ's redemption."[63]

62. BB, 944.
63. BB, 949.

The Reading of the Word of God follows the Introductory Rites. Two full texts are provided from the Book of Genesis for the reading: the first is a portion of the story of creation, and the second is the account of Adam naming the animals God created. The order of blessing also suggests two additional options, from Genesis and Isaiah; however, the full texts are not provided in the rite. If the blessing takes place on a farm, you might invoke St. Isidore or St. Modestos (Patron Saint of Farm Animals). The second Prayer of Blessing emphasizes that God has "given us care over other living things."[64] "A minister who is a priest or deacon says the Prayer of Blessing with hands outstretched; a lay minister says the prayer with hands joined."[65] The Prayer of Blessing is followed by the option of sprinkling the animals with holy water. Consider this option if it won't cause too much disruption for the pets—dogs especially love the water!

Finally, the liturgy concludes with a final blessing that asks God "to protect and sustain us."[66] A closing song may be sung, contributing to a fuller celebration of this blessing. Many parishes end this celebration with some kind of refreshment and hospitality, being sure to include treats for the pets who have been blessed (and consider the needs of multiple animals). If this is included, it of course calls for hospitality ministers or other volunteers who can assist with the fellowship. A lovely gesture would be to invite those bringing their pets for a blessing to bring donations of pet food, which could then be given to local no-kill animal shelters.

Order for the Blessing of Images for Public Veneration by the Faithful

The Order for the Blessing of Images for Public Veneration by the Faithful is found in chapter 36. Parishes often purchase or receive images (as donations and gifts) that enhance the interior of the church building and contribute to the personal, devotional prayer of the Catholic faithful. Likewise, statues or other images may adorn the church grounds.

The introductory notes for this blessing provide a solid theology of the Catholic practice of venerating sacred images. "The Church encourages the devout veneration of sacred images by the faithful, in order that they may

---

64. BB, 958.
65. BB, 957.
66. BB, 960.

see more deeply into the mystery of God's glory."[67] Although this practice is encouraged, the Church does caution that this is a devotional and personal practice, and it should not take place during Mass. Therefore, the blessing of images is to be celebrated outside of Mass and instead during a Celebration of the Word or within Evening Prayer. A lay person may not preside; the ordinary minister is to be a priest or even a bishop.

Chapter 36 includes three sets of blessings for images: those of Jesus (part I), those of Mary (part II), and those of a saint (part III). The images may include framed icons or other paintings, statues, tapestries, and so on. These blessings are particularly appropriate when the parish erects a new shrine area within the church or adds statues outside on the property.[68] The blessing may take place inside or outside the church, wherever the image is located. Each follows the same order of prayer but with texts that are specific to the three distinct images being blessed. A full complement of liturgical ministers should be available to assist with the celebration: greeters or ushers to help the people assemble, servers to assist the priest, a cantor and accompanist, and trained parish readers. A worship aid should be provided to help the gathered faithful participate. When the blessing takes place outside, be sure to provide microphones and speakers so the assembly can hear the ministers and participate. You may also need to set up a lectern for the proclamation of the readings and intercessions.

The celebration begins with the Introductory Rites: the sign of the cross, a greeting, and an introduction to help those present prepare for the celebration. Note that the greeting for each of the three orders of blessing specifically references the person whose image is being blessed: "the image of the unseen God"; "born of the Virgin Mother"; and "the crowning glory of all the saints." Preparation teams may use these texts or compose their own using "other suitable words, taken primarily from sacred Scripture."[69] The introductions for all three orders of service similarly focus on the person whose image is being blessed.

The Reading of the Word of God follows the Introductory Rites. Each order of blessing provides complete texts for the suggested readings and alternate options. If the alternate options are selected, the readings will need to be prepared in a ritual binder or the *Lectionary for Mass* or *Liturgy of the*

---

67. BB, 1258.

68. Parish teams should note that a separate blessing for Stations of the Cross is found in chapter 42.

69. BB, 1264, 1278, and 1292.

Hours ritual books will need to be used. These suggestions come from a particular mystery of the Lord (that is depicted in the image), the Common of the Blessed Virgin Mary (or proper texts from a feast or memorial associated with the image), or the Common of the Saints (or proper texts associated with the saint in the image), and for each order there is a complete text given for the reading, with other prescribed options as choices.

The reading of Scripture is followed by the psalm. Every effort should be made to ensure that the psalm is sung by the cantor so that the liturgy is a fuller celebration. The ritual text provides the text of the psalm along with other suggested options. Select a setting that is familiar to the assembly.

Each of the three blessings in this chapter allow for intercessions that precede the Prayer of Blessing. The intercessions for each blessing are particular to the one whose image is being blessed, including not only references

Blessings provide a good opportunity to involve school children.

to the person, but also allowing the response to be specific: for an image of Christ, the response may be "Lord, make us like your Son"; for an image of the Blessed Virgin Mary the response may be "Lord, through your Mother's intercession, hear our prayer"; and for an image of a saint the response may be "Through the intercession of Saint. N., save us, O Lord." Of course, all three blessings allow the response to be the well-known "Lord, hear our prayer." The response may be sung. The intercessions would be announced by the deacon, if there is one, or a reader.

The Prayer of Blessing follows the intercessions. As with the intercessions, these blessings are particular to the image being blessed. When an image of Mary is blessed, the image *may* be incensed. Note that the blessings for an image of Mary or of a saint *may* be incensed, whereas incensing an image of the Lord is required in the rubrics. This follows other instances in which specific and symbolic images of the Lord are rightly honored with incense: the altar of sacrifice, the crucifix of the church, the paschal candle, the *Book of the Gospels*, the members of the Body of Christ.

The Prayer of Blessing is followed by a simple Concluding Rite in which people are blessed. A song or hymn that references the person whose image is blessed would be a most appropriate end to the celebration—for example, a hymn to the Lord or a hymn to Mary or a hymn honoring the saints.

Blessings Celebrated outside of Mass and in Other Locations

The *Book of Blessings* includes various blessings that would appropriately be celebrated in a home, school, or other location. Blessings that may be celebrated in the home, for example, are wonderful opportunities for parishioners to experience these liturgies of the Church. Many of the blessings of persons that are found in part I of the *Book of Blessings* may be celebrated in the home—such as the blessing of a

A priest blesses a vineyard in Elgin, Arizona.

family, the blessing of a home, the blessing of a person confined indoors, and so on. These are powerful examples of the Church's pastoral care to the faithful. Therefore, making their availability known to the people of the parish would most certainly help to catechize the faithful about these liturgies and also contribute to a more full experience of the liturgical life of the Church and of the parish.

Other blessings that may appropriately be celebrated in a school, in an office building, or even in a field of crops are addressed here.

Order for the Annual Blessing of Families in Their Own Homes

The Order for the Annual Blessing of Families in Their Own Homes is in part II of chapter 1 of the *Book of Blessings*. The introductory notes emphasize that "pastors must regard as one of their primary pastoral duties the faithful visitation of families to bring the message of Christ's peace."[70]

The Word became flesh and made his dwelling place among us. It is Christ who enlightens our hearts and homes with his love.

—*Book of Blessings*, 1604

---

70. BB, 68.

It strikes a very pastoral tone when it refers to these annual visits by the pastor and his associates as a "sacred trust" and a "rich opportunity to fulfill pastoral responsibilities that grow in effectiveness the more the priests come to know the families."[71] It is noteworthy to consider that even the title of this blessing uses the term "annual," presuming that these visits and this blessing are done on a regular basis. Although the introduction identifies the Easter season as the ideal time for this blessing, the indication is that it may be celebrated at any time of the year, given the limitations of a pastoral staff being able to visit *every* home of the parish within one season. Such pastoral visits might be accompanied by a meal that the family shares with their pastor, associate pastor, or the deacon assigned to the parish.

The introduction to this blessing further notes that while the blessing is ideally celebrated in each individual home, those families that may live in the same building or locale (such as the same neighborhood) may gather in one place, and the blessing would be celebrated with the families gathered together. Along these same lines, the introduction allows for other adaptations that may be needed because of circumstances or the situation, noting that the structure and chief elements of the blessing are to be maintained. The introductory notes also encourage that "the celebrant's manner of presiding at the celebration should manifest the attentive concern of charity toward all present, particularly the young, the elderly, and the sick."[72]

The rubrics presume that the pastor of the parish presides over this blessing; however, the associate pastor and deacon may also preside. Even when presiding in someone's home, the minister should be properly vested in an alb and stole. A lay minister does not preside over this blessing.

The blessing should take place in a room with enough space for everyone in the family to gather comfortably, such as a family room or living room. Enough seats should be provided for everyone participating. The home prayer environment may include a crucifix (if one is not already hanging in the room), a candle, and perhaps a Bible. These items could be placed on a small table in a prominent place in the room, perhaps covered with a nice cloth. It would be appropriate to ask one of the family members to serve as a liturgical minister, especially as a reader and, if he or she is trained, as a server to help the presider.

---

71. BB, 69.
72. BB, 74.

The Introductory Rites include a greeting and an introduction that helps prepare the family to receive the blessing. Although the introduction provided in the rite may be used, the presider may choose to adapt it using similar words. He might want to make it more personal for the particular family. Interestingly, while the rubrics do not recommend the inclusion of an opening song, it does recommend that a closing song be sung. Even so, you could appropriately begin with a song from the familiar repertoire of the parish so that all can easily participate. The family will presumably need the words, so presiders should come prepared with a worship aid (they will also need to know the responses to the service.) Even a familiar psalm refrain could be used. Of course, if a family member plays a musical instrument it would be very fitting that he or she accompany the blessing (if they have access to the music).

The introduction provided in the rite wonderfully illuminates the spirituality and theology of this blessing:

> The purpose of the parish visit is that through the ministry of the priest (deacon) Christ may enter your home to bring you peace and joy. This happens above all through the reading of the word of God and the prayer of the Church.[73]

After the introduction, the Reading of the Word of God takes place. The rubrics direct that one of those present or the celebrant himself proclaim the reading. The ritual provides a full text from the Gospel. In this reading, Jesus speaks about the house that is built on rock. The ritual also provides five other selections. The presider will need access to these texts since they are not found in the *Book of Blessings*. The order of service suggests that Psalm 100 follow with its response: "We are the people: the sheep of his flock."[74] Psalm 128 and 148 are also suggested. Even though this blessing takes place in a family's home, it is still best to sing the psalm. Be sure to select a familiar setting. After the psalm, the celebrant preaches a brief homily to help those present understand the meaning of the celebration.

The Reading of the Word of God continues, as usual, with the praying of intercessions. There are two different sets that can be used: the first is used if the celebration takes place within the Easter season, and the second is used when the blessing takes place at another time of the year. The intercessions found in the ritual may be used or adapted. The response given for the first

73. BB, 76.
74. BB, 79.

set is "Lord, stay with us," which seems very fitting for a blessing of families in their home. The second response is "Lord, make us holy." Of course, the familiar "Lord, hear our prayer" may also be used for either set. The intercessions conclude with the Lord's Prayer, followed by the blessing itself.

With hands outstretched over the family members, the priest or deacon prays one of three texts the ritual provides. The first is for use during the Easter season and uses paschal images. The other two options are for use outside the Easter season. The first asks that God "bestow on this family and this home / the riches of [his] blessing"[75] and the second asks God to "grant that those who live / here may obtain the gifts of the Holy Spirit. / Through their works of charity let them show what grace your blessing gives."[76]

After the Prayer of Blessing, the presider sprinkles those present and the home itself. Some families have the custom of retrieving holy water from the parish's baptismal font and keeping this on hand in the home for personal prayer. The priest or deacon may use this water for the blessing, or he may bring his own holy water. If the priest or deacon does not bring the holy water vessel from the parish, care should be taken that the vessel used to hold the water is appropriate for a liturgical celebration—for example, a clean, attractive glass bowl. The rubrics provide an explanatory text that can be said during the sprinkling, which seems particularly appropriate during the Easter season: "Let this water call to mind our baptism into Christ, / who has redeemed us by his death and resurrection."[77]

The blessing concludes with a simple final prayer and a suitable song. Again, this could be a hymn or refrain that is well known and can be sung a cappella, or accompanied by a member of the family who plays a musical instrument. Consult the parish hymnal for something known that everyone can sing.

Blessing of a New Building Site

The Order for the Blessing of a New Building Site is found in part II of chapter 10. Part II concerns blessings related to buildings and to various forms of human activity. The introductory notes for part II set the stage for the blessings of constructions, such as a new building site (chapter 10), a new home (chapter 11), a new seminary (chapter 12), a new hospital (chapter 17), and other buildings and places (from chapters 10–20). The notes remind us that:

---

75. BB, 85.
76. BB, 86.
77. BB, 87.

Through the guidance of faith, the assurance of hope, and the inspiration of charity the faithful are enabled to discern with wisdom the reflections of God's goodness not only in all the elements of creation but also in all the events of human life. They see all of these as signs of that fatherly providence by which God guides and governs all things."[78]

It's a lovely articulation of our theology and our belief that, indeed, all of life gives us the opportunity to "always and everywhere" give thanks and praise to God for all that he has done for us and continues to do for us. "The orders of blessing contained in part II are provided for the buildings, materials, and other major resources involved in the various activities and pursuits of the faithful."[79]

When blessings are celebrated outside, the presider should still be vested, a dignified place should be prepared for the readings, and a cross should be present (not shown here).

It is important to note here that this order of blessing would not be used in the process of building a new church. Though there is a similar blessing for the building of a new church, it is part of the *Order of the Dedication of a Church and an Altar*. Chapter 1 (part IV) of that ritual text includes the Order of Laying a Foundation Stone or the Commencement of Work on the Building of a Church. This is the ritual to use when blessing the site of a new church building.

The introductory notes for the Order for the Blessing of a New Building Site notes that it is used when breaking ground or laying a cornerstone for "an important new building, especially one to be erected for a particular community,"[80] but in reality this blessing can be used for any building being built. The blessing is presided over by a priest or deacon vested in an alb and stole. In addition to those who will be using the new site, the blessing will take on a fuller meaning if the construction workers are present and able to participate.[81] Be sure to have microphones, speakers, and a lectern for the reading prepared at the site for the liturgy.

---

78. BB, 639.
79. BB, 641.
80. BB, 642.
81. See BB, 644.

The presumption is that the blessing be celebrated outside at the actual construction site. Parish teams will need to consider how this affects the celebration. A full complement of liturgical ministers should be provided according to circumstances and the situation—if possible, a minister of music, a trained reader, and someone to assist the presider. A prepared worship aid would also benefit those who gathered at the blessing.

The *Book of Blessings* rarely specifies a suggested opening or closing song, but it does so for this blessing: a setting of Psalm 127:1–2. If this is not familiar to the community, another suitable song may be selected.

The Introductory Rites include the sign of the cross, a greeting, and text for an introduction that helps prepare the gathered community for the blessing. The presider may choose to write his own text in similar words. Of special note, the rubrics allow for a representative of the construction workers to say a few words about the new building before the presider's introduction.[82]

The Reading of the Word of God follows with the typical structure of a reading followed by a psalm and an opportunity for the celebrant to preach. The order of service provides the text of 1 Corinthians in which St. Paul identifies Christ as the foundation upon which we build. Three other options are given, from Isaiah, 1 Peter, and the Gospel of Luke. If these readings are chosen, a ritual binder or the lectionary will need to be prepared. Responsorial Psalm 121 or 90 follows the reading, although another suitable song may be sung. Given that the format most Catholics are familiar with is a responsorial psalm, this would probably make the most sense. Select a familiar musical setting.

The presider may offer a homily, and then the intercessions are prayed. The petitions provided in the ritual text are specific to the new building site. Parish teams may use these texts but may adapt them or compose new texts. Notice that in this order of blessing the format of the intercessions is different than what usually takes place, at Sunday Mass for example. Rather than petitions imploring God to do something specific for *us*, the petitions are statements of faith that conclude with "Blessed be God for ever." The assembly will probably be more familiar with the invitation to prayer "Let us pray" or "We pray to the Lord." Instead, the statements of faith conclude with "Let us bless the Lord." This is the assembly's cue to respond with "Blessed be God for ever." They will need the invitation and response to be printed in the

---

82. See BB, 648.

worship aid.[83] If other intercessions are composed, be sure to follow the same format as those given in the ritual text.

Two options are provided for the Prayer of Blessing. The presider offers this prayer with his hands outstretched over the construction site. The first option asks that the new site be for God's "glory and our own well-being" and that it "may progress day by day to its successful completion."[84] The second option asks that this new work "contribute / to the spread of the kingdom of Christ."[85]

The order of blessing then allows for the site to be sprinkled with holy water, so if this is determined to be part of the blessing, it will need to be provided for in the preparations for the blessing. A vessel for the holy water and an aspergillum will need to be prepared. Here too is where the laying of the cornerstone takes place, if that is part of the blessing. Since this is a rather involved act of construction, which usually involves the placement of a large block of cement or stone, sometimes using construction equipment, the order of blessing suggests that a suitable song be sung as this is happening. As an option, consider a setting of one of the optional psalms given in the Reading of the Word of God.

After this, the order of blessing provides a threefold blessing over the people, which the celebrant prays with his hands outstretched over the assembly that has participated. The order of blessing concludes with the optional singing of a song or hymn.

Order for Blessing of St. Joseph's Table

The Order for the Blessing of St. Joseph's Table is found in chapter 53 of the *Book of Blessings*. In some places, it is the custom "to bless bread, pastries, and other food and give a large portion of it to the poor" on the Solemnity of St. Joseph, which takes place on March 19. This is a fitting practice and custom, for St. Joseph is the patron saint of the universal Church (the Body of Christ), a body that often suffers in need. Care for the poor is a theme woven throughout the various elements of this order of blessing, and it is one of the few blessings that attach a specific action to it to be performed: here a corporal work of mercy—specifically, to feed the hungry. While no other specification is given as to what foods would be part of the St. Joseph's Table,

---

83. See BB, 645.
84. BB, 655.
85. BB, 656.

many traditions from various cultures of Central and Eastern Europe include additional foods such as fish, eggs, vegetables, and other non-meat dishes, since this solemnity falls within the penitential season of Lent.

This blessing could be a wonderful parish or school celebration that could people together in the latter part of Lent to celebrate God's blessings and provide a communal means of observing one of the traditional Lenten disciplines of giving alms. The blessing might be followed by a simple meal in the parish hall or school cafeteria, and participants might share some of the food that is blessed. It could also be a lovely family celebration preceding the evening dinner on or near the solemnity. During the weeks before St. Joseph's Day, the parish might encourage this family celebration in the parish bulletin, or with the children through the parish school and religious education program. The blessing may be presided over by a priest, deacon, or lay minister.

Every poor, needy, suffering or dying person, every stranger, every prisoner, every infirm person is "the child" whom Joseph continues to protect. For this reason, Saint Joseph is invoked as protector of the unfortunate, the needy, exiles, the afflicted, the poor and the dying.

—*Patris corde*, 5

The blessing can take place in the parish church, but it can also happen in another place of the parish outside the church. For example, a large room in the parish center could be chosen. The rubrics do not provide recommendations for the table itself. Presumably it would be a table large enough to hold the foods being blessed. The table could be covered with a nice cloth with the foods arranged on it. There should be enough room around the table for the presider to approach the food for the blessing.

No matter the circumstances in which the blessing is celebrated, a suitable complement of ministers should be provided: music ministers who lead the singing, trained readers to proclaim the Scripture and announce the intercessions, and greeters and ushers if the celebration is on a parish or school level. Even in a more intimate, family setting these roles should be provided, filled by family members. A worship aid should be provided so that all may participate in the songs and responses.

Once all have gathered, the blessing begins with an opening hymn. Choose something familiar, from the parish repertoire, so that people may easily participate. The hymn is followed by the customary sign of the cross and the greeting. Proper texts and gestures are provided for lay ministers or the ordained. The introduction that follows helps prepare those gathered for the blessing, noting that we honor St. Joseph with the donations of food for the poor, which are a sign of God's abundant blessings. The introduction may be adapted by the presider.

The Word of God is then proclaimed. The full texts of the account of Joseph's dream in Matthew is provided as well as the suggestion for Matthew 13, in which Jesus is identified as "the carpenter's son" (or Joseph's son). If the latter reading is chosen, the presider will need the lectionary or a ritual binder. The reading is followed by a familiar setting of Psalm 89, Psalm 112, or another suitable song. Given that the format most Catholics are familiar with is a responsorial psalm, this would probably make the most sense.

As with many other orders of blessing, the one who is presiding may offer a brief explanation of the Scriptures and of the meaning of the celebration. This would also be a good opportunity to speak about the custom of the St. Joseph's Table, it's tradition, and it's specific connection to our call to serve the poor and the hungry.

The rubrics for this blessing provide a unique alternative option for the typical intercessions. Intercessions are provided, but they may be replaced with the Litany of St. Joseph. This litany follows the usual pattern of a formal litany of the Church, in which first there are petitions for God's mercy, and then invocations for the intercession of St. Joseph that use scriptural and traditional titles for Joseph: Light of Patriarchs, Husband of the Mother of God, Faithful Guardian of Christ, Pattern of Patience, Lover of Poverty, Patron of the Dying, Protector of the Church, and so on. Then the litany concludes with the three-fold invocation to the Lamb of God. Given that this is a celebration in honor of St. Joseph, the second option of the litany might be a suitable choice. Parish teams should be aware that in May of 2021 Pope Francis added seven additional invocations to the Litany of St. Joseph. These additional invocations should be added to what is found in the *Book of Blessings*.[86]

After the intercessions or Litany of St. Joseph, the whole assembly prays the Lord's Prayer, and then the Prayer of Blessing follows. Only one option is given, and it references the many good gifts of God, asks that the food upon the table be blessed, and asks that the prayers of St. Joseph might "sustain us and all our brothers and sisters / on our journey towards [the] heavenly

---

86. The litany may be found here: https://www.fdlc.org/sites/default/files/JosephLitany2021.pdf.

kingdom."[87] If a priest or deacon offers this prayer, he does so with his arms outstretched over the table, whereas a lay minister does so with his or her hands joined.

The Blessing of St. Joseph's Table is a wonderful opportunity to include various ministries in the parish, and even every parishioner. The parish social justice ministry, for example, might organize a food drive in which parishioners are encouraged to donate nonperishable food items. Using announcements at Mass during the preceding weeks, the parish bulletin, the website, and other social media, parishioners could be directed to drop off their food donations at a designated spot in the parish. This food, then, could also be blessed during the celebration and then given to the parish food pantry, or neighborhood food pantry if the parish doesn't have one.

Blessings Celebrated during Morning Prayer or Evening Prayer

Some blessings may take place during the celebration of Morning Prayer or Evening Prayer from the Liturgy of the Hours. In this case, the form of blessing provided in the *Book of Blessings* is adapted. Following the Gospel canticle, the intercessions from the order of blessing are prayed, then the Lord's Prayer, and then the blessing itself. The blessing itself takes place after the Lord's Prayer. The blessing of throats on the optional Memorial of St. Blaise may be celebrated during Morning Prayer or Evening Prayer. This blessing includes the formula provided in the *Book of Blessings* and takes place after the reading and responsory (or homily if one is given) and before the Gospel Canticle.

The rubrics in the order of blessing will indicate whether the blessing may be celebrated during Morning or Evening Prayer and provide the instructions for adapting the order of blessing within this liturgy.

Shorter Form of Blessings

The *Book of Blessings* provides a shorter form for some blessings. Not every blessing includes this form. These shorter forms most often begin with an opening dialogue, followed by a short proclamation of Scripture, which may or may not be followed by a psalm. The Prayer of Blessing follows the Scripture. Missing in these shorter forms are the introductory texts, the

---

87. BB, 1693.

homily or reflection after the readings, intercessions, and the Lord's Prayer. Even if this shorter form of a blessing is used, the proclamation of the Word of God and the Prayer of Blessing itself are never to be omitted.[88] This indicates the Church's regard for these two principle elements of a blessing.

When a shorter form is provided, the rubrics often note that it can be used "in special circumstances."[89] Careful consideration should be given to what constitutes a "special circumstance" that would warrant the use of the shorter form. Certainly, the physical health or condition of people may be a consideration when choosing the shorter form of a blessing. But mere convenience or the desire for brevity should never be part of the equation. The celebration of the full rite should always be the ideal for any liturgy of the Church.

Appendix: Order for the Installation of a Pastor

The installation of a new pastor is a wonderful celebration in the life of a parish. It marks a new and exciting chapter in the life and growth of a parish community of faith. With careful preparation this celebration can be a profound expression of the ministry and service to which we are all called, particularly that of a new parish pastor. The introduction to the order of blessing notes that "it is appropriate that [the new pastor] be publicly installed by a liturgical rite . . . [which] should, if possible, take place at one of the Masses on the first Sunday that his appointment is effective."[90]

The introduction also notes that the installation of a pastor may also take place within a Liturgy of the Word or during Morning or Evening Prayer.[91] Given that this is such an important celebration in the life of a parish, it seems best that it take place at a Sunday Mass, when the largest number of parishioners would be able to participate. Since Mass is the principle celebration in which this rite should take place, it will be discussed in this section.[92]

---

88. See BB, 23.

89. See, for example, the Order for the Blessing of Religious Articles, BB, 1445.

90. BB, 2012.

91. Unlike other forms of blessing that may take place during Morning or Evening Prayer, the rubrics for the installation of a pastor do not provide instructions concerning the adaptation of the rite for these liturgies. It would make sense, however, that the installation be inserted after the Gospel Canticle and conclude with the intercessions.

92. "If the rite of installation is celebrated outside Mass, a liturgy of the word is celebrated. The rite of installation follows the gospel (BB, 2022–2030). The installation rite concludes with a hymn, the general intercessions (see BB, 2031), the Lord's Prayer, and a blessing. The new pastor may briefly address the people before the general intercessions" (BB, 2020).

Celebration at Mass

There are two forms of the installation of a pastor: one for when a bishop presides, and another when a priest presides. While it is ideal that the bishop of the diocese install a new pastor, he may delegate a priest to preside in his place. This priest-delegate would most likely be a vicar or the priest who is the dean of the area in which the parish is located.

When the bishop presides, he is the principle celebrant of the Mass, and the priest to be installed as pastor concelebrates. If the bishop has delegated a priest to preside, then that priest greets the people at the beginning of the Mass and presides over the installation of the new pastor. However, the new pastor then becomes the principle celebrant for the remainder of the Mass, beginning with the opening collect (see below).

More often than not, the installation of a new pastor includes many guests and visiting clergy—for example, neighboring pastors or priest-friends of the new pastor. Care and preparation should go into providing for all those who may not be familiar with the parish and into providing vesting information and instructions to the clergy regarding the liturgy.

Regarding seating, the introduction to the order of installation notes that the parish council, and possibly the parish trustees if there are any, should be seated in the front of the church, as they will be presented to the new pastor during the installation. Likewise, other clergy of the parish and the parish staff are presented to the new pastor, so arangements for the seating of all these groups should also be attended to.

These groups may also be in the opening procession of the Mass. If this is the case, the order of the procession might be: thurifer, processional cross and candles, parish staff, parish trustees, parish council members, followed by the lectors, deacon with the *Book of the Gospels*, concelebrating priests, pastor-elect, and finally, the bishop.

There are no special Mass texts or readings for the installation of a pastor, so the Mass of the Day is used.

When a Bishop Presides

When the bishop is present the order of installation begins after the proclamation of the Gospel. After the Gospel has been read, the pastor-elect stands before the bishop. Presumably this would be in the front of the sanctuary so that all are able to see. Speaking to the faithful of the parish, the bishop says, "My dear friends, because I am aware of your pastoral needs and am confident in Father N.'s qualifications for the office of pastor, I now commend Father N. to you as your new pastor,"[93] a very simple, but a profound commendation in which the pastor being installed is literally presented to the parish by the bishop. The order notes that other words may be used or the words given may be adapted.

The people show their approval and support of the new pastor, which is most often in the form of applause. Of course another expression could be used. For example, the liturgical assembly could sing a short acclamation such as "Thanks be to God" or "Praise and thanks to you, Lord." After their show of approval, all are seated for the bishop's homily.

Following the homily, the pastor-elect once more stands before the bishop, who presents to him the other parish clergy and the members of the parish pastoral staff. The new pastor is encouraged to "share this ministry [the pastoral care of the people of the parish] in a spirit of mutual trust, common prayer, and genuine concern."[94] If the pastoral staff is seated in the front of the church, members can easily come forward to greet the new pastor individually, or they could be invited to stand at their places. Keep in mind that this may involve people already being in the sanctuary—for example, the associate pastors or deacons. If a musical acclamation was sung after the people welcomed the new pastor, they might sing the same acclamation after the presentation of the clergy and staff.

The bishop then presents the parish council to the new pastor, reminding the pastor that the council "is the voice of your people and will assist and counsel you as you minister in this parish."[95] Again, this might be followed by the same sung acclamation. If it seems appropriate, the new pastor may greet each of the members of the parish council. If there are parish trustees, they may be presented to the pastor. The bishop reminds the pastor that they "will share with you the responsibility for the parish's corporate and legal affairs."[96]

In a rather powerful demonstration of his role as shepherd, teacher, and leader, the pastor then leads the whole liturgical assembly in the profession of the Nicene Creed. Following the creed, the pastor addresses the bishop with an oath of fidelity.

---

93. BB, 2022.
94. BB, 2026.
95. BB, 2027.
96. BB, 2028.

The universal prayer follows. It should include an intercession for the new pastor, the pastoral leadership, and indeed the whole parish at this special time in its life. The order of service provides sample intercessions as well as the introduction and concluding prayer. The Mass continues in the usual way; however, the newly installed pastor may address the parish following the prayer after Communion.[97]

When a Priest Presides

When the pastor is installed by another priest (such as the vicar of priests or dean), the installation rite takes place at the beginning of the Mass. After the greeting, the pastor-elect stands before the priest who has been delegated to preside at the installation. Another priest (such as a neighboring pastor or another dean) presents the pastor-elect, noting that "after consulting with the clergy and laity of the diocese, Bishop N. has chosen the Reverend N. as the new pastor of this parish."[98] The priest delegate responds, reminding the people that the bishop "has asked me to express, in his name, his pastoral concern for the people of this parish, and he commends Father N. to you as your new pastor."[99]

The people express their approval and support of the new pastor, and the installation rite continues as described above—all within the Introductory Rites. Once the presentations have taken place, the priest delegate admonishes the new pastor to "always be a loving father, a gentle shepherd, and a wise teacher of your people, so that you may lead them to Christ who will strengthen all that you do."[100] The new pastor then takes his place at the celebrant's chair and prays the collect. From this point on he is the principle celebrant of the liturgy. The universal prayer may be offered as found in the rite or adapted.[101]

---

97. See BB, 2019.

98. BB, 2034.

99. BB, 2035.

100. BB, 2041.

101. The appendixes of the *Book of Blessings* also include a series of solemn blessings and prayers over the people. Refer to page XX for more information.

Frequently Asked Questions

1. What is the difference between blessing, commissioning, and consecrating?

Blessing refers to the direct act of praising God and then asking for his favor on a particular person (for example, one who is sick) or thing (for example, the Oil of the Sick). *Commissioning* (or *mandating*) is usually an act of delegation where one is charged with a specific action (for example, distributing holy Communion during Mass or taking holy Communion to the sick). Commissioning may include a blessing. *Consecrating* is a unique form of blessing in which the Father is asked to send the Holy Spirit upon a specific person (for example, one being ordained a bishop) or thing (for example, the sacred chrism, or the elements of the Eucharist, or a new altar) in order that the Holy Spirit might sanctify the person or thing.

The late Cardinal George blesses the new office space of Liturgy Training Publications in 2009.

2. Who can bless?

Some blessings are reserved to ordained ministers (bishops, priests, or deacons) and are usually those items that are blessed for use in the liturgy, for the devotional life of the people, or a specific item related to the church building. The *Book of Blessings* notes that the priest is the appropriate presider in these instances "especially [at those blessings] that involve the community he is appointed to serve."[1] The *Catechism of the Catholic Church* also clarifies the role of the ordained: "[T]he more a blessing concerns ecclesial and sacramental life, the more is its administration reserved to the ordained ministry."[2] Some blessings are reserved to the specific order of minister. For example, a new *cathedra* (the bishop's chair in every cathedral) can only be

---

1. BB, 18b.
2. CCC, 1669.

blessed by the bishop. This makes sense, given it is "a preeminent sign of the teaching authority belonging to each bishop in his own Church."[3] However, the *Book of Blessings* also notes that "in virtue of the universal priesthood, a dignity they possess because of their baptism and confirmation,"[4] a layman and laywomen may preside at certain orders of blessings. It will be clarified in the rubrics of particular blessings when lay ministers may preside (for example, the blessings of a family, parents after the birth of a child, various means of transportation, fields and flocks, and others).

3. Is it appropriate for the priest celebrant to invite the assembly to join him in a communal blessing?

The ritual books of the Church are very specific about the gestures and postures of those in the liturgical assembly. The rubrics direct appropriate gestures for both the ministers and the gathered faithful. The *Book of Blessings* never directs the faithful to extend their hands in blessing along with the presider. In fact, the *Book of Blessings* is very specific that a lay presider should join his or her hands instead of extending the hands over the object or person that is to be blessed. Because of this, it would not be appropriate for the entire liturgical assembly to extend their hands in a gesture of blessing.

4. How might a parish determine when it is appropriate to celebrate a blessing during Mass?

The *Book of Blessings* determines whether it is appropriate for a blessing to be celebrated during Mass. The order of blessing itself will provide rubrics and a special order of prayer for this purpose. If the order of blessing does not provide the option for the blessing to take place during Mass, then it should be presumed that doing so is not appropriate and are not allowed (for example, the Blessing of a St. Joseph's Table on March 19).

For orders of blessing that may be celebrated during Mass, pastoral considerations will help determine which ones to celebrate and how often they might occur. Some blessings are associated with the sacramental life or the communal life of the Church, and so might be more obviously joined to the celebration of the Mass. For example, the Orders for Blessing New or Departing Parishioners seems more appropriately celebrated within the

---

3. BB, 1153.
4. BB, 18d.

Sunday Mass, since that is when the greater number of parishioners are gathered together and can welcome the new parishioner or send well-wishes to one who is departing.

Since Sunday Mass is the primary liturgical celebration of the parish, those who prepare the liturgy should take care that this celebration includes blessings from time to time. While the weekly inclusion of blessings could add an undue burden to the Sunday Mass, periodic celebrations on Sundays will enrich the sense of the liturgical life of the parish and foster a greater awareness of Catholic sacramentality.

5. I thought that blessings always included the sprinkling with holy water. Is this not the case?

It's probably a surprise to you, but yes, blessings do not always include the sprinkling with holy water. The "General Introduction" explains the use of the outward signs of blessings, of which their purpose is to "bring to mind God's saving acts, to express a relationship between the present celebration and the Church's sacraments, and in this way to nurture the faith of those present and move them to take part in the rite attentively."[5] Aside from the gesture that the minister makes while offering the Prayer of Blessing ("the outstretching, raising, or joining of the hands, [or] the laying on of hands" the introduction specifies the sign of the cross, the sprinkling with holy water, and incensation. A careful review of the rubrics will inform you as to which sign is used. And in some cases, the addition of the specified sign is optional.

6. How may parish ministers encourage families to use *Catholic Household Blessings and Prayers*?

Catholic Household Blessings and Prayers is a collection of prayers developed by the United States Conference of Catholic Bishops (USCCB). It is to be used specifically by the faithful in the dioceses of the United States. In its introduction, the bishops conference encourages families to use these blessings and prayers frequently: "Make it part of family dinners and holiday celebrations, of bedtime routines and special occasions."

The more that parishioners are familiar with the celebrations of blessings, the occasions that warrant them, and the rhythms of prayer that they create in the life of the parish, the more apt they might be to celebrate them

---

5. BB, 25.

Parents may sign their child's forehead with the sign of the cross in an act of blessing.

in their own homes with their own families. As blessings are introduced and established as a common form of liturgical prayer in the parish, so they may be introduced into the life of the domestic Church. Frequent reminders from parish leadership of seasonal blessings could help families make these celebrations a more common experience of family prayer (for example, the Advent wreath, the Christmas tree, and the nativity). These reminders can take the form of parish bulletin articles about blessings or articles on the parish website. A parish might make a concerted effort to make known *Catholic Household Blessings and Prayers*, and even provide information on how families can order it from the USCCB or other distributers.

7. When the sprinkling rite occurs during Easter Time, the priest should use the water blessed at the Easter Vigil. Is it appropriate for the priest to rebless the water?

The Roman Missal provides the rite of blessing and sprinkling with holy water. The missal presumes that during Easter Time the water for the sprinkling rite is the same water that was blessed at the Easter Vigil for baptism and the renewal of baptismal promises. Because the water was already blessed, it is not re-blessed on the succeeding Sundays of Easter in which the sprinkling rite occurs. Instead, the *Rite of Christian Initiation of Adults* provides a prayer of thanksgiving (as opposed to a Prayer of Blessing) for the water.[6] This prayer does exactly what its title indicates—it thanks God for the gift of the water that has already been blessed and will now be used as a reminder of our baptism. The only time this water would be blessed for the sprinkling rite is if the water used is not that which was already *blessed* at the Easter Vigil.

This is similar to the Rite of Anointing of the Sick. The rite first provides a prayer of thanksgiving over the oil of the sick because it presumes that the priest is using the oil that has already been blessed by the bishop at the annual

---

6. See RCIA, 222D and E.

Chrism Mass. Only secondly does it provide a Prayer of Blessing in case the priest is using oil that wasn't already blessed by the local bishop.[7]

8. If the parish or a person is in need of a blessing that does not have an official order of service what can be done?

The final chapter in the *Book of Blessings* (chapter 71) includes the Order for a Blessing to be used in Various Circumstances. The rubrics note that the purpose of this blessing is to be used in those situations in which a blessing has not been provided. Additionally, this blessing may be adapted to suit the specific situation. It follows the usual format of an Order of Blessing: Introductory Rites, Reading of the Word of God, Prayer of Blessing, and Concluding Rite. Adapting this rite is a wonderful opportunity to include special blessings particular to a local community.

9. Are there blessings that are not found in the *Book of Blessings* but approved for use?

There are other blessings that are part of the Church's liturgical life that are not found in the *Book of Blessings*. For the most part, these blessings are celebrated within the celebration of an annual Mass or are part of the celebration of specific sacraments. Sixty-five blessings are part of the celebration of specific sacraments—for example, the blessing of ashes or palms, the blessing of the rings during a wedding, or the blessing of parents during a baptism.

The *Rite of Christian Initiation of Adults* also includes the Blessings of the Catechumens,[8] which duplicates what is already found in chapter 4, part III, of the *Book of Blessings*.[9] *Pastoral Care of the Sick* also includes the rites for visiting the sick (adults and children) in chapters 1 and 2. These rites include a blessing for the person who is ill, but the order of prayer and the included texts differ from those in the *Book of Blessings* in chapter 2, part I.

Since the publication of the *Book of Blessings* in 1989, a handful of blessings have either been newly composed or retranslated. In 2007, the United

---

7. See *Pastoral Care of the Sick: Rites of Anointing and Viaticum*, 123.

8. See RCIA, 95.

9. Parish teams should take note that at the time of this publication, the *Rite of Christian Initiation of Adults* is being retranslated. The second edition of this rite will include an updated translation of the Blessing of Catechumens. The title of the ritual text will be the *Order of Christian Initiation of Adults*.

States Conference of Catholic Bishops received approval from Rome for the *Order of Blessing on the Fifteenth Birthday.* This blessing has existed for quite some time and is popular among Catholics of Latin America and other Latino/Latina communities. It is the celebration of the *Quince Años* (fifteenth birthday) which marks a young woman's transition from childhood into adulthood.[10] In the dioceses of the United States it has gained in popularity such that the bishops decided to formally adopt the ritual for use in this country. Similarly, in 2012, the bishops of the United States received approval from Rome for the *Rite for Blessing a Child in the Womb.* This blessing was created in order to support parents who await the birth of a child and to foster respect for life in the womb. It is also available as a bilingual (English and Spanish) supplement from the USCCB. Both this blessing and Order of Blessing on the Fifteenth Birthday are available as bilingual editions (English and Spanish) from the United States Conference of Catholic Bishops.

Blessings are part of every sacramental celebration, such as the blessing of rings during the Order of Celebrating Matrimony.

In 2016, Rome approved the English translation of the *Order of Celebrating Matrimony,* second edition, for use in the dioceses of the United States. In this second edition, the appendix includes revised translations of the Order of Blessing an Engaged Couple and the Order of Blessing a Married Couple within Mass on the Anniversary of Marriage. These replace the rituals found in the current *Book of Blessings.* The rubrics in these orders of blessing have been clarified, and in some instances changed. If these are celebrated in the parish, the texts should come from the *Order of Celebrating Matrimony* (appendixes II and III).

In addition, the *Order of Blessing the Oil of Catechumens and of the Sick and of Consecrating the Chrism* was newly translated in 2018. The previous translation had been available in the appendixes of the former *Sacramentary* and in the *Roman Pontifical.* The *Book of Blessings* currently includes the Order for the Blessing of a Chalice and Paten (within Mass and within a celebration of the Word of God). The celebration within Mass had previously

---

10. See the appendix in this resource.

been found in the *Sacramentary*. However, an updated text was prepared with the new translation of the third edition of *The Roman Missal*. The new translation of the celebration within Mass is found in appendix IV of the missal. Although it is preferable that this celebration take place within Mass (and using the texts found in the missal), it may still take place during the Liturgy of the Word. Use the *Book of Blessings* for this purpose, but update the proper responses (for example, "And with your spirit").

10. How does the third edition of The *Roman Missal* and other new translations of ritual books and prayers affect the *Book of Blessings*?

The third edition of *The Roman Missal* was promulgated in 2011. This new edition of the missal included a new translation for the doxological ending of all collects. No longer do prayers end with "We ask this through Christ our Lord" or "Grant this through Christ our Lord." Instead, the ending is a simple statement: "Through Christ our Lord." Since the publication of the missal, the Congregation for Divine Worship and the Discipline of the Sacraments (a Vatican office) issued the decree that "one God" should be omitted from the fuller doxological endings of prayers. This means that collect prayers will end with "Through our Lord Jesus Christ your Son, who lives and reigns with you in the unity of the Holy Spirit / God, for ever and ever. / Amen." The *Book of Blessings* was first issued in English in 1989. A new translation has yet to be prepared, so it includes the former doxological endings. When using this ritual text, presiders should update the endings to correspond with the missal. *The Book of Blessings* also retains the former response "And also with you." The assembly's response should be updated to correspond with the missal, "And with your spirit."

Chapter 1 of the current *Book of Blessings* also includes the Orders for the Blessing of a Married Couple (chapter 1, part III) and the Order for the Blessing of an Engaged Couple (chapter 1, part VI). The newly translated *Order of Celebrating Matrimony* (2016) includes an updated translation (which affects texts and rubrics) in its appendix. The new translation of these blessings supersedes those found in the *Book of Blessings* and should be used in practice.[11]

The Litany of St. Joseph is found in the Blessing of Saint Joseph's Table (chapter 53). This Litany was originally approved in 1909 and has been a rich

---

11. See also question #8.

part of the devotional life of the Church. On May 1, 2021, the Memorial of St. Joseph the Worker, Pope Francis approved the addition of seven new invocations drawn from "modern papal texts about St. Joseph." It is hoped that the new invocations will "increase our love for this great saint . . . [and] encourage us to implore his intercession and to imitate his virtues and his zeal."[12] The texts were only published in Latin, and it is up to individual conferences of bishops to provide translations for their country. The United States Conference of Catholic Bishops provides the English translation of the new invocations on their website (https://www.usccb.org/prayer-and-worship /prayers-and-devotions/litanies/litany-of-saint-joseph). These may be used in the Blessing of Saint Joseph's Table.

---

12. As quoted by Catholic News Service on May 2, 2021; available here: https://catholicreview. org/vatican-approves-new-invocations-for-litany-of-st-joseph/.

APPENDIX:
ORDER FOR THE BLESSING ON
THE FIFTEENTH BIRTHDAY

The United States Conference of Catholic Bishops has published additional blessings that are apart from the *Book of Blessings*. Among these blessings is the *Order for the Blessing on the Fifteenth Birthday* (*Bendición al cumplir quince años*). This bilingual, English and Spanish, ritual was published by the USCCB in 2007. "Among several Spanish-speaking countries and among many Latinos/Latinas in the United States there is the custom of celebrating the passage from childhood to adolescence with a ritual that expresses thanksgiving to God for the gift of life and that asks for a blessing from God for the years ahead."[1]

This celebration is commonly referred to as the *Quinceañera. Quince años* is more proper (and in line with the actual title of the ritual text). Technically speaking, the term *quinceañera* refers to the girl who celebrates her fifteenth birthday (from *quince* meaning "fifteen," and *añera*, a girl marking years [*años*]), and the celebration itself is the *Fiesta de Quince Años*, or fifteenth birthday celebration.[2] In common usage, *Quinceañera* is a broader term, referring to the girl, the liturgy, and the party that often follows.[3]

Hispanic or Latino parents place a high degree of importance in celebrating their daughter's fifteenth birthday, which is an expression of her development into a young woman. Their little girl is no longer a child and is entering adolescence. The *Quince años* might be equated with a "sweet sixteen" in American popular culture. In some elite social circles, the debutante ball is the celebration in which young ladies are formally introduced into society. In south Texas and other places along the US-Mexico border, one might hear a reference to a "debut." One important distinction between the

---

1. *Order for the Blessing on the Fifteenth Birthday* (OBFB), 1.
2. Pastoral ministers should note that the rubrics use the word *quinceañera* to refer specifically to the girl who is celebrating her birthday.
3. For the purposes of this chapter, the author will use the term from the ritual text.

Quince años and a debutante ball is that the *Quince años* is understood to have two components: a liturgical celebration, then a party. This celebration is, for many families, and expression of their Catholic faith. This dimension is not taken lightly.

The purpose of the blessing on the fifteenth birthday is for family and friends to give thanks to God for the gift of life and to ask for God's blessing and guidance upon the girl in the years to come. In this celebration, the girls who are celebrating their fifteenth birthday will offer a prayer in which they thank God for "creating [her] in his image and likeness / and for calling [her] to be [his] daughter through Baptism."[4] She continues to thank God for the gift of his Son, and she asks for his grace to help her be committed to the Christian life as a young woman and modeling this life for others.

The act of blessing calls for the baptized girl to be more like Jesus.

The *Quince años* liturgy is usually celebrated on, or as close as possible to, the actual birthday. This is not a sacramental celebration, and in terms of precedence for scheduling may be considered an option subject to the discretion of the pastor and the parish schedule. The *Order for the Blessing on the Fifteenth Birthday* indicates that the liturgy is from the Mass of Thanksgiving in the Masses for Various Needs and Occasions.[5] Your local ordo will indicate the days on which the Masses for Various Needs and Occasions are permitted. For example, a *Quince años* celebration is not celebrated during Holy Week. This may be an opportunity to catechize the parents, the young lady, and other members of the family and friends about the liturgical year, and about the way we observe and pray through the liturgical year. The ritual text does provide two options for the liturgical celebration: within Mass or outside of Mass.

---

4. OBFB, 8.
5. See OBFB, 3.

Quince Años within Mass

When the *Quince años* takes place during Mass, the Introductory Rites and the Liturgy of the Word take place as usual. The readings "may be taken either from the *Lectionary for Mass* or from the Mass of Thanksgiving in Masses for Various Needs and Occasions."[6] Following the Gospel, a brief homily follows. After the universal prayer (sample texts are provided in the rite[7]), the Liturgy of the Eucharist is celebrated in the usual manner, including the distribution of Communion. "Before the final blessing the priest invites the *quinceañera(s)* to make an act of thanksgiving and of a personal commitment to lead a Christian life."[8] The *quinceañera* may recite the words given in the ritual booklet, or one in similar words—that is, something she writes. When writing her own thanksgiving, the young lady may receive guidance from a parish catechist or liturgist to help her articulate the promises she will make when reciting this prayer. The priest then receives her act of thanksgiving. He may silently sprinkle the girl with holy water, and the girl may be invited to place flowers before an image of the Blessed Virgin Mary. Godparents or other sponsors may give the girl gifts of religious articles, such as a Rosary, Bible, or medal. These items should be blessed before the liturgy (parishes should use the Order for the Blessing of Religious Articles [chapter 44] or the Order for the Blessing of Rosaries [chapter 45] as found in the *Book of Blessings*). "At the end of the Mass" the girl (or girls) is blessed with a special prayer and then the final blessing of the assembly occurs in the usual way. The rite recommends that the closing song should "suitably express . . . thanksgiving and joy."[9] The Magnificat is suggested.

Loving God,
you created all the people of the world
and you know each of us by name.
We thank you for these quinceañeras,
who today celebrate their fifteenth birthday.
Bless them with your love and friendship
that they may grow in wisdom,
knowledge, and grace.
May they love their family always and
faithful to their friends.
Through Christ our Lord.
Amen.

—Prayer of Blessing
Order for the Blessing on the Fifteenth Birthday, 14

---

6. OBFB, 3.
7. See OBFB, 33–34.
8. See OBFB, 8.
9. OBFB, 16.

Quince Años outside of Mass

A priest or deacon may preside over the *Quince años* when it takes place outside of Mass. The celebration may begin with an entrance procession with an accompanying gathering song; or the song is sung after everyone has gathered. After the sign of the cross and the greeting, the Liturgy of the Word takes place. There is no collect. Instead the presider offers an introduction to the celebration which includes the invitation for the assembly to be seated to listen to the Word of God.[10]

There is only one reading. The rite recommends Jeremiah 1:4–10; however, another reading may be chosen.[11] There is no indication in the ritual text that the presider should offer a homily. Instead, the girl's prayer of thanksgiving follows the reading. Just as at Mass, the priest receives her act of thanksgiving, and he may sprinkle the girl with holy water and then invite her to place flowers before an image of the Blessed Virgin Mary. The godparents and sponsors may present their blessed gifts. The presider offers a special blessing over the girl and then invites the congregation to offer one another a sign of Christ's peace. A joyful song, such as the Magnificat may end the celebration.

Parish Coordination

Some parishes have *Quince años* coordinators, similar to a wedding coordinator. This person helps the parents and the girl work out ahead of time who will be in the procession; who will sit where (daughter with one parent on either side, or daughter alone with parents in front pew); who will proclaim the Word (along with instructions about approaching and leaving the ambo); who will bring the gifts of bread and wine during the preparation of the gifts; who will help in the distribution of Communion; where the Communion stations are in that particular sanctuary; as well as who will be in the recessional and the order of these persons. The coordinator also runs a rehearsal usually the day before the actual celebration. The coordinator might also help those in attendance understand the rubrics of the Mass: when to stand, when to sit or kneel, when to process, sometimes even go over the responses of the Mass and set up the expectations for singing and responding aloud. It is a great time for liturgical catechesis with a captive audience. In addition to all this,

---

10. See OBFB, 17–20.
11. OBFB, 21.

many parishes prepare detailed worship aids that promote the participation of the assembly in all these varied ways.

Ministers for a *Quince Años*

The presider, in the case of a celebration within Mass, is a priest or even a bishop. It would be appropriate in the case of a celebration outside of Mass that the presider be a deacon. Most parents, if not all, want the celebration of Mass, not only a Liturgy of the Word with or without Communion. Lay ministers may not preside.

Just as in any liturgical celebration, well-prepared ministers include readers, altar servers, extraordinary ministers of holy Communion (the number depending on the projected number of worshippers), and music ministers, including instrumentalists and a well-trained cantor. When a large number of worshippers are expected, ministers of hospitality are also highly encouraged.

The selection of liturgical ministers should not be seen simply as a way of acknowledging the friendship or familial ties between the girl and the person chosen. Readers must be well suited and prepared to proclaim the Scriptures selected. Perhaps if they are youth who participate in regular parish ministry, this might be a place to start. Their lack of experience as parish readers should not preclude them from being invited, always keeping in mind that they possess the most basic pronunciation skills so that the Word of God is heard clearly and strongly.

If the *quinceañera* is formed and trained as a parish reader, she may be invited to offer the Scripture reading at the celebration.

Altar servers should already be trained and know what is required for this ministry. Because each priest has certain preferences in the manner that altar servers serve at Mass, and also taking the variety of worship spaces into consideration, it is best to choose servers from the parish who are familiar with and comfortable in the space. Since this ministry requires specific training and preparation, it is advisable that younger siblings or friends not be invited to fill this ministry simply for the sake of giving them a way to be involved if they have never served at Mass.

Care must be taken in the selection and invitation of extraordinary ministers of holy Communion. Generally speaking, invite family members or friends who are already commissioned as extraordinary ministers in their own parishes, or ask the pastor for a one-time commission for specially selected persons. It is important to follow diocesan guidelines when selecting these liturgical ministers, especially if they come from another parish or from out of town.

Music should be done in the manner customary in a given parish. Try to avoid celebrations that are devoid of music, for one way that the people participate is by means of singing hymns, psalms, and responses in addition to the spoken responses. It may be necessary to engage parish musicians much as one would do for a wedding, including offering them a stipend for this service. Some parishes have strict liturgical music protocols, closely following the norms for liturgical celebrations. Music for this celebration should be prepared and approved well in advance. A minimum of six weeks is strongly advised. Some parishes may require as much as three months in advance of the celebration.

The girl and her family may invite other family members or friends to be ministers of hospitality. Hospitality ministers welcome guests to the celebration. A smiling, friendly demeanor are qualities to look for. Remind them that they are not there merely to pass out worship aids.

Baptismal godparents and grandparents play an important role in witnessing to the life of this young lady. If at all possible, they should be invited to be present and to participate in the ritual at the appointed time.

Liturgical Environment

Some parishes have strict liturgical environment guidelines that apply not only to *Quince años* celebrations, but also to weddings. Once the environment team has carefully prepared the church for a liturgical season, moving or changing the environment might not be allowed. This fifteenth birthday celebration takes place within the context of the particular liturgical season. Within Lent or Advent, additional floral arrangements might be allowed with moderation but removed at the end of the celebration. Ideally, almost any arrangements may be used during Ordinary Time, still within the parish guidelines for number and size. During Christmas Time and Easter Time, the liturgical environment is usually festive enough not to warrant additional floral enhancements. Generally speaking, families do not spend a large percentage of their budget for this party on flowers. It would be fitting for the Paschal candle to be lit during Easter Time.

Because it is traditional for there to be "gifts" to be blessed, there should be some type of credence table for said "gifts." These may include a Bible, a rosary, a prayer book, or a religious medal, but don't be surprised if the family wants to include a tiara, a necklace, a ring, a bracelet, and "the last doll." Not all *quinceañeras* choose to have these gifts at their celebration. Include the giving of the religious articles within the liturgical celebration. Remember that these religious items should be blessed beforehand. Help the parents and the young lady to understand that these particular religious items have a future spiritual use in her life: her praying of the Rosary, her reading of Scripture from her Bible, her wearing of her medal or a scapular. Encourage the parents who wish to present non-religious gifts to the young lady to do this at the party to follow: the donning of the tiara and the presentation of the ring, necklace, bracelet, earrings. Another option is that she receive these gifts at home before the celebration of the liturgy, and only the religious articles be blessed and presented at church.

Music

Some parishes have the advantage of working with the *quinceañera* and her parents to select the music for her celebration. A young lady who is committed to faith formation and youth ministry in her parish might already come to this session with some concrete ideas for repertoire. Expect to be pleasantly surprised.

Since prelude music prepares the assembly for the worship of God, the sources should be from the body of sacred music, not secular songs. The latter can be saved for performance at the party or reception.

In general, look for songs expressing thanksgiving or joy, life with Christ at the center, or songs expressing commitment to mission and discipleship, particularly as closing songs. Just as at Sunday liturgy, sing the responsorial psalm, Gospel acclamation, Sanctus, memorial acclamation, Amen, and Agnus Dei. Consider psalms of praise for the responsorial psalm. A musical setting of the Magnificat can serve as either a closing hymn or a hymn to accompany the presentation of flowers to the Blessed Mother. In order to facilitate the participation of the assembly, consider familiar settings of all the music, and engage the ministry of a cantor or song-leader.

Worship Aids

It is strongly recommended that a worship aid be prepared in order to encourage the participation of the people. A simple worship aid might give the order of worship with references to song numbers from a parish hymnal, and a more elaborate worship aid might include the music to the hymns, or at least words only. It is important to include the appropriate copyright acknowledgments and obtain a license to reprint the words and music if the parish does not already have a parish license to do this.

Joint Celebrations

Joint celebrations of the *Quince años* are not unheard of. Several young ladies, along with all their families and friends, may celebrate together at one liturgy. Some parishes might designate specific dates on their parish calendars—for example, quarterly—at which several families celebrate together closest to the date of the birthday.

Working with Families

Catechists and liturgical ministers play a special role in working with families (parents, godparents, and sometimes the siblings come along as well). Help them understand that all liturgy belongs to the Church as a whole, not to individuals or private groups. The liturgy is a ritual that helps us worship God by hearing God's Word, offering thanksgiving, receiving Christ's Body and Blood in the Eucharist, making a commitment to living as disciples, and receiving a blessing. The liturgy is already planned for us. What we need to do is not plan, but rather prepare the elements of the liturgy. It is not up to individuals to modify the liturgy to their liking. The catechist or a liturgical minister can help the young lady reflect on the Scriptures in order to select the ones that most resonate with her. This is a great opportunity to help her and her family to do *lectio divina* on the Scriptures she has chosen by means of handouts that include reflection questions. Help her reflect on her own baptism, appreciate the beauty and privilege of receiving the Eucharist, and reflect on the meaning of commitment for the years ahead, including mission and discipleship in the world. You will also need to work with the families to determine what language to use. Will only Spanish be used? English?

Or will the liturgy be bilingual? Help the families consider the primary needs of those attending the liturgy.

Financially, many parents spare no expense when it comes to this celebration. It can be seen as a mini-wedding. There is a saying in Spanish, "*echaron la casa por la ventana*" ("They threw the house out through the window"), meaning that they go into debt just to give their daughter the party of her dreams. Celebrations can quickly become elaborate and expensive, from formalwear to limousines to a multi-tiered cake and a high-tech DJ and light show. These often include extended family who fly in from other states or countries, as well as a broad group of school mates. Encourage parents to exercise restraint and balance. You might go so far as to ask them to consider making a contribution to the poor from what they choose to save in their budget.

Parish Involvement

As stated earlier, all liturgical celebrations belongs to the entire Church. Socially, some celebrations are not perceived this way. *Quince años* celebrations are often considered private events, just as weddings are considered private events, in the sense that one invites very specific guests to attend. Encourage families to open the celebration to the rest of the parish community.

In the same way that parishes might celebrate the baptism of infants at Mass, or the celebration of the rites of the catechumenate at different weekend liturgies, one way to involve a larger segment of the parish is to encourage families to have a *Quince años* celebration at one of the regularly scheduled weekend Masses. Ideally, because of the ensuing party, this could be the anticipated Sunday Mass on Saturday evening. This works particularly well when the girl desires a very simple celebration. The girl sits with her parents and the rest of her family, even extended family. Special kneelers should not be put out for her, especially if they were to be placed in front of the altar, as at many weddings. Encourage the family to sit among the assembly. The young lady might be invited to be one of the readers if she is well prepared or suited for this ministry. Or her family might be selected to bring up the gifts of bread and wine at the presentation of gifts. After Communion, she might be invited forward to receive the blessing.

Particularly in parishes with larger Latino/Latina membership and attendance, the parish youth minister can create awareness of these important celebrations in the lives of these young ladies. One must also be aware of the fact that some young ladies approaching this birthday do not wish to have this celebration. It helps to know that it is optional, not a social/cultural requirement. In some parishes, once or twice a year (depending on numbers) there might be mini-retreats for the girls nearing this celebration. They can invite the members of their courts, including non-Catholics, to spend a day in prayer and song, and hold catechesis about the tradition and its symbolism and the importance of this passage in the life of a young person. This is a wonderful catechetical opportunity for young Catholics who are not strong in their faith or in their participation in worship or catechesis. It's also an opportunity for interfaith prayer and for the introduction of Catholic liturgy to others.

RESOURCES

Ritual Books and Church Documents

- *Bendicional*: The Mexican edition of the *Book of Blessings*. It may be used in the dioceses of the United States.

- *Blessing of the Oils and the Consecration of Chrism*: Ritual that contains the official blessings for the oil of catechumens and the sick as well as the consecration of the Chrism that take place during the annual Chrism Mass. Formerly in the *Roman Pontifical*, this new translation is available as a separate ritual book from the USCCB (2019).

- *Book of Blessings*: The practice of blessing is an ancient and worthy tradition in the Church, and the blessings in this collection express the belief of the Church that every good gift comes from God, who sanctifies all people and all created things. Abridged and shorter editions are available from Liturgical Press in addition to the regular ritual edition.

- *Built of Living Stones*: This document from the United States Conference of Catholic Bishops provides general norms for the liturgical environment.

- *Catholic Household Blessings and Prayers*: This ritual book was prepared by the United States Conference of Catholic Bishops specifically for use by Catholic families. It provides a wonderful collection of rituals adapted to seasons and particular days in the liturgical year and includes blessings that families may do at home. A new softcover edition was made available in 2020. The Canadian equivalent is *Blessings and Prayers for Home and Family* (Canadian Conference of Bishops).

- *Ceremonial of Bishops*: This document provides the rubrics and directions for celebrating the rites with a bishop, including the blessing of an altar, chalice and paten, a baptistry or new font, a new cross and bells, and of a cemetery.

- *Directory on Popular Piety and the Liturgy*: This document provides a rich treasury of information about particular Catholic customs and devotions including blessings.

- *Lectionary for Mass*: The lectionary includes a variety of readings that can be used in multiple situations, including blessings.

- *Order for the Blessing on the Fifteenth Birthday*: This bilingual ritual (English and Spanish) was approved for use in the diocese of the United States and published in 2009 for celebrating a young woman's transition into adolescence on their fifteenth birthday.

- *Order of Celebrating Matrimony*: The newly translated ritual text for celebrating Matrimony includes an appendix with the blessing of engaged couples and the blessing of married couples on significant anniversaries. The retranslated texts replace those that are currently found in the *Book of Blessings*.

- *Prayers against the Power of Darkness*: A pocket-sized ritual book for individuals seeking to protect themselves against evil. It includes extracts from *Exorcisms and Related Supplications* that may be used by those who are not appointed to the ministry of exorcist. It is available from USCCB Publishing (2017).

- *Rite for the Blessing of a Child in the Womb*: In 2008, the United States Conference of Catholic Bishops published the approved bilingual (English and Spanish) ritual for blessing a child in the womb. It is not found in the *Book of Blessings*.

- *Rite of Christian Initiation of Adults*: This ritual book used for the initiation of new Catholic Christians includes the blessing of catechumens.

- *The Roman Missal*: Although the missal is primarily used for the celebration of Mass, it does include newly translated texts for the blessing of a chalice and paten.

- *Sacrosanctum concilium*: As the first document of the Second Vatican Council, this resource provides the context upon which all other liturgical documents and ritual texts should be understood.

- *Sing to the Lord: Music in Divine Worship*: This document from the United States Conference of Catholic Bishops provides general norms for preparing liturgical music in the United States.

Theological and Historical Resources

- Chupungco, Anscar J., ed. *Handbook for Liturgical Studies, Volume IV: Sacraments and Sacramentals.* Collegeville, MN: Liturgical Press, 1997. This extensive encyclopedia-like resource provides a detailed study of the sacraments and sacramentals of the Catholic Church.

- Chupungco, Anscar J. *Liturgical Inculturation: Sacramentals, Religiosity, and Catechesis.* Collegeville, MN: Liturgical Press, 1995. A discussion on the relationship between liturgy and culture.

- Deiss, Lucien, CSSP. *Springtime of the Liturgy.* Translated by Matthew J. O'Connell. Collegeville, MN: Liturgical Press, 1979. This classic, written by one of the pioneers of the liturgical renewal movement, presents a detailed study of early Christian rituals through the fifth century.

- Simons, Thomas G. *Blessings: A Reappraisal of Their Nature, Purpose, and Celebration.* Saratoga, CA: Resource Publications, 1981. "This resource provides the basis for a renewed theology to help restore blessings to a role of keeping with their rich contribution to prayer through the ages." Although this work is out of print, older copies may be found online, in libraries, or in theological bookstores.

Pastoral Resources

- *The Catholic Handbook for Visiting the Sick and Homebound.* Chicago: Liturgy Training Publications. Published annually, this is the essential resource for lay ministers of care, especially extraordinary ministers of holy Communion. It includes the official rites from the *Book of Blessings* and *Pastoral Care of the Sick: Rites of Anointing and Viaticum* to bring holy Communion to, and pray and share the Gospel with, those who cannot regularly worship with their parish community.

- Jeep, Elizabeth McMahon. *Blessings and Prayers through the Year: A Resource for School and Parish.* Chicago: Liturgy Training Publications, 2007. This beautiful hardcover book offers numerous prayers, blessings, and rituals for all of the occasions and needs that arise in both school and parish life. The book has a clear, easy-to-follow format and offers helpful background information and ideas for preparing for ritual and prayer. Included are two CDs, one with music and vocals to teach the songs and the other with musical accompaniment only. There are also music pages for teaching and playing in groups. Classes can begin using this valuable resource at any time during the year.

- Reed, Elizabeth Hoffman. *Giving Thanks at the Table*. Chicago: Liturgy Training Publications, 1999. This book for families includes a collection of quotes and blessings for mealtime. The selections are arranged according to specific days and seasons of the year. There are also prayers for before or after meals at any time of the year.

- Rosetti, Stephen J. *The Priestly Blessing: Rediscovering the Gift*. Notre Dame, IN: Ave Maria Press, 2018. A historical and pastoral overview of Catholic blessings.

- *Sourcebook for Sundays, Seasons, and Weekdays*. Chicago: Liturgy Training Publications. Published annually, this resource includes pastoral notes for celebration the various blessings through the liturgical year.

GLOSSARY

Acclamation: A brief, joyful liturgical response, such as "Amen" or "Blessed be God!"

Alb: A full-length white liturgical robe, from the Latin *albus*, meaning "white." The alb is the preferred vestment for all ministers, from server to bishop. It recalls the white garment put on at baptism as a sign of putting on the new life of Christ. Ordained ministers wear a stole and an outer garment over the alb.

Aspergil (Aspergillum): The liturgical object used to sprinkle holy water.

Aspersorium: The small bucket or vessel that holds holy water and that can be carried for the purpose of sprinkling the assembly. Sometimes the sprinkler (*aspergil*) is called the aspersorium as well.

Benediction: From Latin, meaning "to bless." Generally, any blessing is a benediction, but the term is also used for the rite that includes a solemn blessing with the Blessed Sacrament at the end of a period of exposition and adoration. The rite also includes Scripture readings, hymns, and silence.

Berakah: A Hebrew prayer form that blesses God, usually beginning with "Blessed are you, Lord our God, King of the universe." This is the basic style of the Hebrew grace after meals, the *birkat ha-mazon*, which seems to be the ancestor of the Christian Eucharistic Prayer.

Blessing: Any prayer that praises and thanks God. In particular, blessing describes those prayers in which God is praised because of some person or object, and thus the individual or object is seen to have become specially dedicated or sanctified because of the prayer of faith. Many blessing prayers ask God's favor toward a person in time of need or on a special occasion. Liturgical celebrations usually conclude with a blessing pronounced over the assembly.

Censer: Another name for a thurible.

Commissioning (extraordinary ministers): A term used for the authorizing and blessing of individuals to function as extraordinary ministers of holy

Communion. It may also be used in a general sense for the blessing or authorization of laypersons to function in any liturgical ministry.

Consecrate: To make holy and set apart through prayer. The term is specifically used at Mass in reference to the bread and wine, which by consecration become the Body and Blood of Christ; at the Chrism Mass in reference to the sacred Chrism; and in the *Roman Pontifical*, in the rite titled "Consecration to a Life of Virginity." In the past, the ordination of a bishop was referred to as a consecration, but the term is not used in the current Rite of Ordination. It is still retained, however, in canon 379 of the 1983 *Code of Canon Law*.

Cope: A long, cape-like vestment. It may be worn in processions joined to a Mass (for example, the procession with palms on Palm Sunday) or at more solemn liturgical celebrations that occur outside Mass (for example, the Liturgy of the Hours or Benediction). The cope is normally worn only by an ordained minister.

De Benedictionibus: The Latin title of the *Book of Blessings*. The Latin text is part of the Roman Ritual (see below).

Exorcism: A prayer or command given to cast out the presence of the devil. The *Order of Baptism of Children* includes a prayer of exorcism, which takes place after the Litany of the Saints. The *Rite of Christian Initiation of Adults* includes prayers of exorcism as part of the rites belonging to the period of the catechumenate and as part of the scrutinies. There is a Rite of Exorcism for use in the case of possession; it may be used only with the express permission of a bishop and only by mandated priest-exorcists.

Final Blessing: A blessing given at the conclusion of a liturgy. It may take the form of a simple blessing, a solemn blessing, or a prayer over the people.

Holy Water: Water that has been blessed. Holy water is usually found in stoups, or fonts, at the entrances of churches so that individuals may bless themselves with it, reminding them of the waters of baptism. It is also used when blessing objects and people. In many churches, a large, covered container of holy water is kept so that the faithful may take some home for devotional use.

Incensation: The act of honoring an individual or an object with incense. This can be accomplished by a minister swinging the smoking thurible (censer) in front of a person, or in front of or around an object, or by allowing the smoke to rise from a brazier placed in front of an object.

Litany: A form of prayer in which a standard response is given to a series of invocations.

Minister: Anyone who serves the worshipping community by performing some function in the liturgy or assisting others in performing theirs. The ordained clergy are referred to as "sacred ministers" in order to distinguish them from the non-ordained ministers in a liturgy. A non-ordained person that has a presiding role is referred to as "another minister" in the ritual text.

Nuptial Blessing: The blessing imparted to a newly married couple at the celebration of the sacrament of matrimony.

Roman Ritual: The title encompassing all the individual ritual books that contain the prayers and rites for the celebrations of the sacraments, other liturgies, and blessings. In general, the Roman Ritual contains all the rites except Mass, which is found in *The Roman Missal*; the Liturgy of the Hours, also called the Divine Office; and those used primarily by a bishop, which are found in the *Roman Pontifical*. Prior to the revision of the rites after the Second Vatican Council, the entire Roman Ritual was contained in one book.

Sacramentals: Sacred signs, including words, actions, and objects that signify spiritual effects achieved through the intercession of the Church. Unlike the sacraments, which have been instituted by Christ, sacramentals are instituted by the Church. Sacramentals include blessings, medals, statues and other sacred images, palms, holy water, and many devotions, including the Rosary. They prepare us to receive the fruit of the sacraments and sanctify different circumstances of life.

Signs: Anything that points to a meaning beyond itself. The meanings associated with signs are mainly literal or informative; they often take their meaning by common consent. For example, an octagon by convention and, eventually, adoption by law, has come to mean that one is required to stop, even though it has no inherent relationship to traffic or movement. Especially in liturgical use, sign is often distinguished from symbol. Symbols are understood to reveal deeper, even ultimate, meaning. Even so, the two terms are often used interchangeably.

Solemn Blessing: The form of blessing in which the standard Trinitarian formula is usually preceded by three invocations. The assembly responds to each of these invocations with "Amen." Formulas for solemn blessings to be used at Mass are given in *The Roman Missal*.

Thurible: A vessel in which incense is burned on coals; also called a *censer.*

Thurifer: The liturgical minister who carries and swings the thurible during liturgies; also called a *censer bearer.* As a ministerial role, it is assigned to an instituted acolyte or other altar server.